SHAKESPEARE
AND
MUSIC

SHAKESPEARE
AND
MUSIC

by
Edward W. Naylor

Published by

Da Capo Press & Benjamin Blom, Inc.

New York
1965

*This unabridged republication of the revised 1931 edition
is printed by special arrangement with
J. M. Dent & Sons Ltd.*

Library of Congress Catalog Card Number 65-16244

Printed in the United States of America

SHAKESPEARE AND MUSIC

(See page xi)

Photograph taken at South Kensington (Victoria and Albert)
Museum, 1895

SHAKESPEARE AND MUSIC

WITH ILLUSTRATIONS FROM THE MUSIC
OF THE 16TH AND 17TH CENTURIES

BY

EDWARD W. NAYLOR, Mus. D.

Honorary Fellow of Emmanuel College
University Lecturer in Music
at Cambridge
Hon. A.R.C.M.

NEW EDITION

LONDON AND TORONTO
J. M. DENT AND SONS LTD.
NEW YORK: E. P. DUTTON & CO. INC.

ALL RIGHTS RESERVED
PRINTED IN GREAT BRITAIN AT
THE TEMPLE PRESS, LETCHWORTH, HERTS
FIRST PUBLISHED IN 1896
REVISED EDITION (RESET), 1931

PREFACE TO REVISED EDITION OF 1931

REVISION of a book after so long an interval as thirty-five years presents difficulties. After consideration, the author has decided that the individuality of the work should not be destroyed by re-writing. Necessary corrections have been made, and some interesting additions supplied.

Most of the instruments in the frontispiece may be seen at the Victoria and Albert Museum, South Kensington.

Canon Galpin has kindly allowed the use of several plates from his book, *Old English Instruments of Music*, published by Messrs. Methuen & Co. Ltd. They are his own photographs from specimens in his well-known collection.

I wish to thank Mr. Charles Lee for his kindly and efficient help in revision, and for interesting suggestions.

E. W. N.

Cambridge, *January* 1931.

PREFACE TO THE FIRST EDITION

This book contains little that is not tolerably well known both to Shakespeare scholars and musicians who have any acquaintance with the history of music. It is hoped that it may be of some use to a large class of students of Shakespeare who have no opportunity to gather up the general information which will be found here. The author also ventures to believe that some brother musicians will be gratified to see at one view what a liberal treatment the great Poet has given to our noble art. It will be observed that settings of Shakespearian songs of a later date than the generation immediately succeeding Shakespeare's death are not noticed. The large number of settings of the eighteenth century, by such men as Arne, though interesting musically, have nothing whatever to do with the student of Shakespeare and the circumstances of his time. It can only be regretted that so much of the original music seems to have perished.

The author is greatly indebted to Mr. Aldis Wright, who has kindly looked through the work in MS., and contributed one or two interesting notes, which are acknowledged in the proper place.

E. W. N.

London, *March* 1896.

CONTENTS

LIST OF PLATES

DESCRIPTION OF FRONTISPIECE

In the middle, on table

QUEEN ELIZABETH'S VIRGINAL. Outside of case is covered with red velvet. Inside finely decorated. Has three locks. The case not, as usual, square, but pentagonal. Compass four octaves and more, for the low B key hints of a "short octave," where the low C♯ would be tuned to a more useful note, viz. AA. So the queen would be able to play Tomkins's *Pavan* or his *Barafostus' Dream*, in the Fitzwilliam Book.

Above the virginal

1. A BOW OF MODERN SHAPE.
2. A BOW OF ANCIENT SHAPE, with no screw.
3. TENOR VIOL. English, late seventeenth century. Observe the sloping shoulders. Six strings, seven frets, plain head.
4. TREBLE VIOL. Label inside says, "Andreas (?) Amati, Cremona, 1637." Observe carved head and flat back.
5. SMALL SIZE FRENCH VIOL. Seventeenth century. Observe the flat back, and shoulder set at angle.
6. TREBLE CORNET. Tube slightly curved, external shape octagonal, bore conical. Cupped mouthpiece made of horn, six holes, and another behind for thumb. Lowest note A, under treble staff.
7. SMALL TABOR-PIPE. Modern, but similar to the Elizabethan instrument. It is a whistle, cylindrical in bore, with three holes, two in front, one behind. The scale begins on the first harmonic, and so is high in pitch. The three holes are sufficient, as the player proceeds to

the second harmonic, etc.   It was played with left hand
only, the tabor being hung on the left wrist, and beaten
with a stick in the right hand.   Length over all of the
pipe in this picture, 14½ inches; speaking length, 13½
inches.   Lowest note in use is B flat *above* the treble staff.
Father Mersenne (1648) says the tabor-pipe was in G,
which makes it larger than the one in the picture.   This
is confirmed by a woodcut of William Kemp (contemporary of Shakespeare) dancing the morris to tabor
and pipe.   (See Calmour's *Fact and Fiction about Shakespeare*.)   Here the pipe seems about eighteen inches
long, which agrees with Mersenne.   A similar woodcut
in *Orchèsographie* makes the pipe even longer.   Both
represent the pipe as conical, like an oboe.   The length
of the tabor, in these two woodcuts, seems about one
foot nine inches, and the breadth, across the head, nine
or ten inches.   There is no "snare" in the English
woodcut, but the French one shows a "snare."

Standing on the floor

1. BASS VIOL, or VIOL-DA-GAMBA, or DIVISION VIOL (a
   smaller size).   Italian, 1600.   Carved head, inlaid finger-
   board, carved and inlaid tailpiece.   Six strings, seven
   frets.
2. LUTE.   Italian, 1580.   Three plain holes in belly, obliquely.
   Ornamental back, flat head.   Pegs turned with key,
   from behind.   Twelve strings.   Ten frets.
3. ARCH-LUTE.   Italian, seventeenth century.   Eighteen
   strings: eight on lower neck, ten on the higher, off the
   fingerboard.   The latter are "basses," half of them
   duplicated.   Seven frets on neck, five more on the belly.

INTRODUCTORY

A PRINCIPAL character of the works of a very great author is, that in them each man can find that for which he seeks, and in a form which includes his own view.

With Shakespeare, as one of the greatest of the great, this is pre-eminently the case. One reader looks for simply dramatic interest, another for natural philosophy, and a third for morals, and each is more than satisfied with the treatment of his own special subject.

It is scarcely a matter of surprise, therefore, that the musical student should look in Shakespeare for music, and find it treated of from several points of view, completely and accurately.

This is the more satisfactory, as no subject in literature has been treated with greater scorn for accuracy, or general lack of real interest, than this of music.[1]

This statement will admit of comparatively few exceptions, one of which must here be mentioned. The author of *John Inglesant*, J. H. Shorthouse,

[1] See my *Poets and Music* (Dent), pp. 33–44, where many names of well-known authors are given, with examples.

whether he "crammed" his music or not, has in that book given a lively and quite accurate picture of the art as practised about Charles I's time.

There is no need here to name the many well-known writers who have spoken of music with a lofty disregard of facts and parade of ignorance which, displayed in any other matter, would have brought on them the just contempt of any reviewer.

The student of music in Shakespeare is bound to view the subject in two different ways, the first purely historical, the second (so to speak) psychological.

As for the first, the most superficial comparison of the plays alone, with the records of the practice and social position of the musical art in Elizabethan times, shows that Shakespeare is in every way a trustworthy guide in these matters; while, as for the second view, there are many most interesting passages which treat of music from the emotional standpoint, and which clearly show his thorough personal appreciation of its higher and more spiritual qualities.

Hamlet tells us, and we believe, often without clearly understanding, that players are *the abstracts and brief chronicles of the time*, and that the end of playing, both at the first and now, was, and is, to hold the mirror up to nature, and *to show the very age and body of the time, his form and pressure.*

The study of this one feature of the "age and body" of Shakespeare's time, with the view of clearly grasping the extreme accuracy of the "abstract and brief chronicle" to be found in his works, will surely go some way to give definiteness and force to our ideas of Shakespeare's magnificent grip of all other phases of thought and of action.

The argument recommends itself: "If he is trustworthy in this subject, he is trustworthy in all."

To a professional reader at all events, it argues very much indeed in a writer's favour, that the "layman" has managed to write the simplest sentence about a speciality, without some more or less serious blunder.

Finally, no Shakespeare student will deny that some general help is necessary, when Schmidt's admirable *Lexicon* commits itself to such a misleading statement as that a virginal is a kind of small pianoforte, and when a very distinguished Shakespeare scholar has allowed a definition of a viol as a six-stringed guitar to appear in print under his name.

Out of thirty-seven plays of Shakespeare, there are no less than thirty-two which contain interesting references to music and musical matters *in the text itself*. There are also over three hundred stage directions which are musical in their nature, and these occur in thirty-six out of thirty-seven plays.

The musical references in the text are most commonly found in the comedies, and are generally the occasion or instrument of word-quibbling and witticisms; while the musical stage directions belong chiefly to the tragedies, and are mostly of a military nature.

As it is indispensable that the student of Shakespeare and Music should have a clear idea of the social status and influence of music in Shakespearian times, here follows a short sketch of the history of this subject, which the reader is requested to peruse with the deliberate object of finding every detail confirmed in Shakespeare's works.

MUSIC IN SOCIAL LIFE

(*Temp. sixteenth and seventeenth centuries*)

Morley, *Plain and Easy Introduction to Practical Music*, 1597, pp. 1 and 2. Here we read of a supper-party, or "banket," at which the conversation was entirely about music. Also—after supper —*according to custom*—"parts" were handed round by the hostess. Philomathes has to make many excuses as to his vocal inability, and finally is obliged to confess that he cannot sing at all. At this the rest of the company "wonder"—and some whisper to their neighbours, "How was he brought up?" Philomathes is ashamed—and goes to seek Gnorimus the music-master. The master is surprised to see him—as Philomathes has heretofore distinguished himself by inveighing against music as a "corrupter of good manners, and an allurement to vices." Philomathes' experience of the supper-party has so far changed his views that he wishes as soon as may be to change his character of Stoic for that of Pythagorean. Thereupon the master begins to teach him from the very beginning, "as though he were a child."

Then follows a long lesson—which is brought to an end by Philomathes giving farewell to the master as thus: "Sir, I thanke you, and meane so diligently to practise till our next meeting, that then I thinke I shall be able to render you a full account of all which you have told me, till the which time I wish you such contentment of mind and ease of body as you desire to yourselfe [Master's health had been very bad for long enough] or mothers use to wish to their children." The Master replies: "I thanke you: and assure your selfe it will not be the smallest part of my contentment to see my schollers go towardly forward in their studies, which I doubt not but you will doe, if you take but reasonable pains in practise."

Later on in the Third Part (p. 136) Philomathes' brother Polymathes comes with him to Gnorimus foɪ a lesson in descant—i.e. the art of extemporaneously adding a part to the written plain-song.[1] This brother

[1] See Appendix.

had had lessons formerly from a master who carried a plain-song book in his pocket, and caused him to do the like; "and so walking in the fields, hee would sing the plaine song, and cause me to sing the descant, etc." Polymathes tells us also that his master had a friend, a descanter himself, who used often to drop in—but "never came in my maister's companie . . . but they fell to contention . . . What? (saith the one), you keepe not time in your proportions: you sing them false (saith the other), what proportion is this? (saith hee), sesqui-*paltery* (saith the other): nay (would the other say), you sing you know not what, it shoulde seeme you came latelie from a Barber's shop, where you had *Gregory Walker* [derisive name for 'quadrant pavan,' 'which was most common 'mongst the Barbars and Fidlers'] or a *curranta* plaide in the new proportions by them lately found out, called sesqui-*blinda*, and sesqui-*harken-after*."

(These mocking terms, sesqui-*paltery*, sesqui-*blinda*, and sesqui-*harken-after*, are perversions of names of "proportions" used in the sixteenth century—as, sesqui-*altera* [3 equal notes against 2].)

We find, on page 208, that both Philomathes and Polymathes are young university gentlemen—looking forward hereafter to be "admitted to the handling of the weightie affaires of the common wealth."

The lessons end with their request to the master

to give them "some songes which may serve both to direct us in our compositions, and by singing them recreate us after our more serious studies."

Thus we find that in Elizabeth's reign it was the "custom" for a lady's guests to sing unaccompanied music from "parts," after supper; [1] and that inability to take "a part" was liable to remark from the rest of the company, and indeed that such inability cast doubt on the person having any title to education at all.

We find that one music-master was accustomed to have his gentleman pupils so constantly "in his company" that they would practise their singing while "walking in the fields."

Finally — that part-singing from written notes, and also the extempore singing of a second part (descant) to a written plain-song, was a diversion of such young university gentlemen, and was looked on as a proper form of recreation after hard reading.

In the sixteenth century music was considered an *essential* part of a clergyman's education. A letter from Sir John Harington to Prince Henry (brother of Charles I) about Dr. John Still, Bishop of Bath and Wells, 1593–1608, says that no one "could be admitted to *primam tonsuram*, except he could first *bene le bene con bene can*, as they called it, which is to

[1] Cf. Rabelais, *Gargantua*, chap. xxiii, where the supper-party "après graces rendues s'addonnoient à chanter musicalement."

read well, to conster [construe] well, and to *sing well*, in which last he hath good judgment." (The three *bene's* are of course *le-gere, con-struere, can-tare*.)

Also, according to Hawkins (*History of Music*, p. 367), the statutes of Trinity College, Cambridge, founded by Henry VIII, make part of the Examination of Candidates for Fellowships to be in *Quid in cantando possint*; indeed, *all members were supposed capable of singing a part in choir service.*[1]

(Long before this, in 1463, Thomas Saintwix, *doctor in music*, was elected Master of King's College, Cambridge.)

Accordingly, we find Henry VIII, who, as a younger brother, was intended for the Church, and eventually for the See of Canterbury, was a good practical musician. Erasmus says he composed offices for the Church. An anthem, "O Lord, the maker of all things," is ascribed to him; and Hawkins gives a motet in three parts by the king, "Quam pulchra es."

Chappell's *Old English Popular Music* gives a passage from a letter of Pasquaglio, the Ambassador-

---

[1] This statement of Hawkins's seems a little exaggerated. Mr. Aldis Wright tells me that the statutes provided for an examination in singing for candidates for fellowships, and that ability gave a candidate an advantage, in case of equality. Singing was not required of all candidates, but the subject was considered on the fourth day of the examination, along with the essay and verse composition.

extraordinary, dated about 1515, which says that Henry VIII "plays well on the lute and virginals, sings from book at sight," etc. Also in vol. i are given two part-songs by the king, "Pastyme with good companye" and "Wherto shuld I expresse." [1]

A somewhat unclerical amusement of Henry VIII's is related by Sir John Harington (*temp.* James I). An old monkish rhyme, "The Blacke Saunctus, or Monkes Hymn to Saunte Satane," was set to music in a canon of three parts by Harington's father (who had married a natural daughter of Henry VIII); and King Henry was used "in pleasaunt moode to sing it." For the music and words, see Hawkins, pp. 921 and 922.

Anne Boleyn was an enthusiastic musician, and, according to Hawkins, "doted on the compositions of Jusquin and Mouton, and had collections of them made for the private practice of herself and her maiden companions."

It appears from the Diary of King Edward VI that he was a musician, as he mentions playing on the lute before the French Ambassador as one of the several accomplishments which he displayed before that gentleman, 19 July, 1551.

There is also a letter from Queen Catherine (of Aragon), the mother of Queen Mary, in which she

---

[1] See my book, *Shakespeare Music* (Curwen), p. 64, for Henry VIII's vocal trio, "Grene growith ye holy."

exhorts her "to use her virginals and lute, if she has any."

As for Elizabeth, there is abundant evidence that she was a good virginal player.

The best-known MS. collection of virginal music (that in the Fitzwilliam Museum at Cambridge) was formerly known as Queen Elizabeth's Virginal Book, and the following quaint story is from Melville's *Memoirs* (1660):

"The same day, after dinner, my Lord of Hunsdean drew me up to a quiet gallery that I might hear some music (but he said he durst not avow it), where I might hear the queen play upon the virginals. After I had hearkened a while I took by [aside] the tapestry that hung before the door of the chamber, and stood a pretty space, hearing her play excellently well; but she left off immediately so soon as she turned her about and saw me. She appeared to be surprised to see me, and came forward, seeming to strike me with her hand, alledging she was not used to play before men, but when she was solitary to shun melancholy." (Queen Elizabeth's virginal is in South Kensington Museum.)

To go on with the royal musicians (who are interesting as such, because their habit *must have set the fashion of the day*), in James I's reign we find that Prince Charles learnt the viol-da-gamba from Coperario (i.e. John Cooper). Also Playford (*temp*. Charles II) says of Charles I that the king "often appointed the service and anthems himself in the Royal Chapel; "and would play his part exactly well on the bass-violl"—i.e. the viol-da-gamba.

George Herbert, who was by birth a courtier, found in music "his chiefest recreation," "and did himself compose many divine hymns and anthems, which he set and sung to his lute or viol. . . . His love to music was such, that he went usually twice every week . . . to the cathedral church in Salisbury; and at his return would say that his time spent in prayer and cathedral music elevated his soul, and was his heaven upon earth." But not only was the poet-priest a lover of church music, for (Walton's *Life* goes on) "before his return thence to Bemerton, he would usually *sing and play his part at an appointed private music meeting*." This was fourteen years after Shakespeare's death.

Anthony Wood, of Merton College, Oxford (1647–51), gives a most interesting account of the practice of chamber music for viols (and even violins, which, by Charles II's time, had superseded the feebler viols) in Oxford. In his *Life*, he mentions that "the gentlemen in privat meetings, which A. W. frequented, play'd three, four, and five Parts with Viols, as, Treble-Viol, Tenor, Counter-Tenor, and Bass, with an Organ, Virginal, or Harpsicon joyn'd with them: and they esteemed a Violin to be an

Instrument only belonging to a common Fidler, and could not endure that it should come among them, for feare of making their Meetings to be vaine and fidling." Wood went to a *weekly meeting* of musicians in Oxford. Amongst those whom he names as "performing their parts" are four Fellows of New College, a Fellow of All Souls, who was "an admirable Lutenist," "Ralph Sheldon, Gent., a Rom. Catholick . . . living in Halywell neare Oxon, admired for his smooth and admirable way in playing on the Viol," and a Master of Arts of Magdalen, who had a weekly meeting at his own college. Besides the amateurs, there were eight or nine professional musicians who frequented these meetings. This was in 1656, and in 1658 Wood gives the names of over sixteen other persons, with whom he used to play and sing, all of whom are Fellows of Colleges, Masters of Arts, or at least members of the university. Amongst them was "Thom. Ken of New Coll., a Junior" (afterwards Bishop Ken, one of the seven bishops who refused to publish the Declaration of Indulgence), who could "sing his part." All the rest played either viol, violin, organ, virginals, or harpsichord, or were "songsters."

"These did frequent the Weekly Meetings, and *by the help of public Masters of Musick*, who were mixed with them, they were much improved."

There seems to have been little that was not pure

enjoyment in these meetings. Only two persons out of the thirty-two mentioned seem to have had any undesirable quality—viz. Mr. Low, organist of Christ Church, who was "a *proud* man," and "could not endure any common Musitian to come to the meeting"; and "Nathan. Crew, M.A., Fellow of Linc. Coll., a Violinist and Violist, *but alwaies played out of Tune.*" This last gentleman was afterwards Bishop of Durham.

Thus we find that in the sixteenth and seventeenth centuries a practical acquaintance with music was a regular part of the education of both sovereign, gentlemen of rank, and the higher middle class.

We find Henry VIII composing church music, and at the same time enjoying himself singing in the three-part canon composed by his friend, a gentleman of rank.

We find that a Fellow of Trinity at the same time was expected to sing "his part" in chapel as a matter of course. We find Edward VI, Mary, and Elizabeth to have all been capable players on lute or virginals. We find that it was the merest qualification that an Elizabethan bishop should be able to sing well; and that young university gentlemen of birth thought it nothing out of the way to learn all the mysteries of both prick-song (a *written* part) and descant (an *extempore* counterpoint), and to solace their weary hours by singing "in parts."

Immediately after Shakespeare's time, we find a courtier of James I, and the ill-fated Prince Charles himself, both enthusiasts in both church and chamber music; and lastly, two years after the regicide, we find the University of Oxford to have been a perfect hotbed of musical cultivation. Men who afterwards became bishops, archdeacons, prebendaries, besides sixteen fellows of colleges, and sundry gentlemen of family, were not ashamed to practise chamber music and singing to an extent which really has no parallel whatever nowadays.

There is plenty of evidence, though more indirect in kind, that the lower classes were as enthusiastic about music as the higher. A large number of passages in contemporary authors shows clearly that singing in parts (especially of "catches") was a common amusement with blacksmiths, colliers, cloth-workers, cobblers, tinkers, watchmen, country parsons, and soldiers.

In Richard Edwards's *Damon and Pythias*, 1565, Grimme, the *collier*, sings "a bussing [buzzing] base," and two of his friends, Jack and Will, "quiddel upon it," i.e. they sing the tune and words, while he buzzes the burden.

Peele's *Old Wives' Tale*, 1595, says: "This *smith* leads a life as merry as a king; Sirrah Frolic, I am sure you are not without some *round* or other; no doubt but Clunch [the smith] can *bear his part*."

Beaumont and Fletcher's *Coxcomb* has:

Where were the *watch* the while? good sober gentlemen,
They were, like careful members of the city,
Drawing in diligent ale, and *singing catches*.

Also in Beaumont and Fletcher's *Faithful Friends*:

Bell. Shall 's have a *catch*, my hearts?
Calve. Aye, good lieutenant.
Black. Methinks a *soldier* [1] should sing nothing else; *catch,
that catch may* is all our life, you know.

(In *Bonduca*, a play of Beaumont and Fletcher's,
altered for operatic setting by Purcell in 1695, there
is a catch in three parts, sung by the Roman
soldiers.)

In Sir William Davenant's comedy *The Wits*,
written in 1633 and published three years later,
Snore, one of the characters, says:

It must be late, for gossip Nock, the *nailman,*
Had catechized his maids, and *sung three catches
And a song*, ere we set forth.

Samuel Harsnet, in his *Declaration of Egregious
Impostures*, 1603, mentions a "merry catch," "Now
God be with old Simeon" (for which see Rimbault's
Rounds, Canons, and Catches of England), which he

---

[1] Drayton (James I's reign) in his *Battle of Agincourt*, line 1199,
has—"The common Souldiers free-mens *catches* sing"—of the
French before the battle (*free*men is a corruption of *three*men).

says was sung by *tinkers* "as they sit by the fire, with a pot of good ale between their legs."

> Now God be with old Simeon
> For he made cans for many a one,
> And a good old man was he, etc.

The tune is given in Byrd's "Hunt's Up," piece lix in the MS. Fitzwilliam Virginal Book at Cambridge; in the printed copy of Breitkopf and Härtel, vol. i, p. 223, section 9. The last lines of the verse are the source of "Ho, jolly Jenkin . . . and troll the bowl to me," in Arthur Sullivan's opera *Ivanhoe.*

And in *The Merry Devill of Edmonton*, 1631, there is a comical story of how Smug *the miller* was *singing a catch* with the *merry Parson* in an alehouse, and how they "tost" the words "*I 'll ty my mare in thy ground,*" "so long to and fro," that Smug forgot he was singing a catch, and began to quarrel with the Parson, "thinking verily, he had meant (as he said in his song) to *ty his mare in his ground.*"

Finally, in *Pammelia*, a collection of rounds and catches of 3, 4, 5, 6, 7, 8, 9, and 10 parts, edited by Thomas Ravenscroft, and published in 1609, there is a curious preface, which states that "Catches are so *generally affected* . . . because they are so consonant to *all ordinary musical capacity*, being such, indeed, as all such *whose love of musick exceeds their skill*, cannot but commend." The preface further asserts that the book is "published only *to please good company*."

To go on to *instrumental* music among the lower classes of Elizabethan and Shakespearian times; there is an allusion in the above-quoted passage from Morley (1597) to the habit of playing on an instrument in a barber's shop while waiting one's turn to be shaved. This is also referred to in Ben Jonson's *Alchemist* and *Silent Woman*. In the latter play, Cutbeard the barber has recommended a wife to Morose. Morose finds that instead of a mute helpmate he has got one who had "a tongue with a tang," and exclaims, "That cursed *barber*! I have married his *cittern* that is common to all men"; meaning that as the barber's cittern was always being played, so his wife was always talking.

There is a poem of the seventeenth century which speaks of the old times:

> In former time 't hath been upbrayded thus,
> That *barber's musick* was most *barbarous*.

However true that may have been—at all events it is certain that in the sixteenth and seventeenth centuries it was customary to hear instrumental music in a barber's shop, generally of a cittern, which had four strings and frets, like a guitar, and was thought a vulgar instrument.[1]

[1] The cittern of the barber's shop had four double strings of wire, tuned thus: 1st, E in 4th space of treble staff; 2nd, D a tone

Another use of instrumental music was to entertain the guests in a tavern. A pamphlet called *The Actor's Remonstrance*, printed 1643, speaks of the *decay* of music in taverns, which followed the closing of theatres in 1642, as follows: "Our music, that was held so delectable and precious [i.e. in Shakespeare's times], that *they scorned to come to a tavern under twenty shillings* salary *for two hours*, now [i.e. 1643] wander with their instruments under their cloaks —I mean, such as have any—into all houses of good fellowship, saluting every room where there is company with, 'Will you have any music, gentlemen?'"

Finally, in Gosson's *Short Apologie of the Schoole of Abuse*, 1587, we find that "London is so full of unprofitable pipers and fiddlers, that a man can no sooner enter a tavern, than two or three cast of them hang at his heels, to give him a dance before he depart." These men sang ballads and catches as well. Also they played during dinner. Lyly says: "Thou need no more send for a fidler to a feast, than a beggar to a fair."

All this leads to the just conclusion, that if ever

lower; 3rd, G on 2nd line; 4th, B on 3rd line. The instrument had a carved head. See *Love's Labour's Lost*, V, ii, 600–3, of Holofernes' head. Also the frontispiece, where the treble viol and viol-da-gamba have carved heads, both human, but of different types. Fantastic heads, as of dragons or gargoyles, were often put on instruments of this type. Cf. Rabelais, II, iii (epitaph on Badebec): "Car elle avoit visage de rebec."

a country deserved to be called "musical," that country was England, in the sixteenth and seventeenth centuries. King and courtier, peasant and plough-man, each could "take his part," with each music was a part of his daily life; while so far from being above knowing the difference between a minim and a crotchet, a gentleman would have been ashamed not to know it.

In this respect, at any rate, the "good old days" were indeed better than those that we now see. Even a *public-house song* in Elizabeth's day was a canon in three parts, a thing which could only be managed "first time through" nowadays by the very first rank of professional singers.

SHAKESPEARE PASSAGES

I

WE now proceed to consider some representative passages of Shakespeare which deal with music.

These may be taken roughly in six divisions—viz.: (1) Technical Terms and Instruments, (2) Musical Education, (3) Songs and Singing, (4) Serenades and other domestic "Music," (5) Dances and Dancing, (6) Miscellaneous, including Shakespeare's account of the more spiritual side of music.

To begin on the first division. There are many most interesting passages which bristle with technical words; and these are liable to be understood by the reader in a merely general way, with the result that the point is wholly or partly missed. With a reasonable amount of explanation, and a general caution to the student not to pass over words or phrases that appear obscure, there is no reason why these passages should not be understood by all in a much fuller light.

The following lines, though not in a play, are so full of musical similes that it may be useful to take them at once.

Rape of Lucrece, line 1124:

> My *restless discord* loved no *stops* nor *rests* ;
> A woful hostess brooks not merry guests.
> *Relish* your *nimble notes* to pleasing ears;
> Distress likes *dumps*, when *time is kept* with tears.

Then to the nightingale:

> Come, Philomel, that sing'st of ravishment,
> Make thy sad grave in my dishevell'd hair:
> As the dank earth weeps at thy languishment,
> So I at each sad *strain* will *strain* a tear,
> And with deep groans the *diapason* bear;
> For *burden* wise I 'll *hum* on Tarquin still,
> While thou on Tereus *descant'st* better skill.
>
> And while against a thorn thou *bear'st thy part*,
> To keep thy sharp woes waking . . .
>
> These means, as *frets* upon an *instrument*,
> Shall *tune* our heart-*strings* to true languishment.

Here Lucrece tells the birds to cease their joyous notes, and calls on the nightingale to sing the song of Tereus, while she herself bears the "burden" with her groans.

The first line contains a quibble on "rests" and "restless" discord. The word "relish" as the name

for an elaborate ornament in lute music, is illustrated
by Colman's example:

Colman was chamber-musician to Charles I. "Nimble
notes" was used in the Shakespearian time as we
should use the term "brilliant music." Lucrece was
in no humour for trills and runs, but rather for dumps,
where she could keep slow time with her tears.
The dumpe (from Swedish dialect, *dumpa*, to dance
awkwardly) was a slow, mournful dance. (See
Appendix.) There is another quibble in line 1131,
on *strain*. A "strain" is the proper Elizabethan
word for a formal phrase of a musical composition.
For instance, in a pavan, Morley (*Introduction to
Practical Music*, 1597) says a "straine" should
consist of 8, 12, or 16 semibreves (we should say
"bars" instead of "semibreves") "as they list, yet
fewer then eight I have not seene in any pauan."

"Diapason" meant the interval of an octave.
Here Lucrece says she will "bear the diapason"
with deep groans, i.e. "hum" a "burden" or drone
in some lower octave than the nightingale's "descant."
The earliest "burden" known is that in the ancient

round, "Sumer is icumen in," of the thirteenth century. Here four voices sing the real music in canon to these words:

> Sumer is icumen in, lhudè sing Cuccu,
> Groweth seed and bloweth mead and springth the wdè nu,
>   Sing Cuccu,
> Awè bleteth after lomb, lhouth after calvè cu,
> Bulluc sterteth, buckè verteth, murie sing cuccu,
>   Cuccu, Cuccu,
> Wel singès thu cuccu, ne swik thu naver nu—

while all the time two other voices of lower pitch sing a monotonous refrain, "Sing cuccu nu, Sing cuccu," which they repeat *ad infinitum* till the four who sing the round are tired. This refrain is called Pes (or "foot"), and this is the kind of thing which Lucrece means by "burden." The word "hum" may be considered technical; see Introductory (p. 14) where "*buzzing* bass" is referred to. The tune, "Light o' Love" (see Appendix), as we know from *Much Ado about Nothing*, III, iv, 41, used to go *without* a burden, and was considered a "light" tune on that account; see *Two Gentlemen of Verona*, I, ii, 80.

"Descant," in line 1134, wants explaining. To "descant" meant to sing or play an *extempore* second "part" to a written melody. The point was that it should be extempore; if written down it ceased to be true descant, and was then called "prick-song." A rough example may be had in the extempore bass or alto which some people still sing in church instead of the melody.[1] A more accurate example of descant would be this—let A sing a hymn tune, say the Old Hundredth, and let B accompany him *extempore* with a separate melody within the bounds of harmony. B is "descanting" on the melody that A sings.[2]

The art of descant in Elizabeth's time corresponded closely with what we call "strict counterpoint" (*contra*, *punctus*, hence "prick-song," or "written" descant).

The modern equivalent for "bear a part" (line 1135) is "sing a part." (See also *Sonnet VIII*.) Any person of decent education could "bear a part" in those days, i.e. read at sight the treble, alto, tenor, or bass "part" of the work presented by the host for the diversion of his guests. (See Introductory.)

Line 1140. "Frets upon an instrument" can still be seen on the modern mandoline, guitar, and banjo. In Shakespeare's days, the viol, lute, and cittern all had frets on the fingerboard, but they were then simply bits of string tied round at the right places for the fingers, and made fast with glue. Their use is

---

[1] Cf. the address "To the Reader" prefixed to Thomas Campion's *Two Books of Ayres* (1613): "Yet do we daily observe, that when any should sing treble to an instrument, the standers by will be offering at an inward part out of their own nature; and, true or false, out it must, though to the perverting of the whole harmony."

[2] Appendix, Ex. 1.

referred to in the next line, to "tune" the strings, i.e. to "stop" the string accurately at each semitone.

There is a quaint illustration of lines 1135–6, about the nightingale singing "against a thorn" to keep her awake, in the words of a favourite old part-song of King Henry VIII's, "By a bank as I lay," where the poem has these lines on the nightingale:

> She syngeth in the thyke;
> And under her brest a pricke,
> To kepe hur fro sleepe.

In close connection with this is the conversation between Julia and her maid Lucetta, in *Two Gentlemen of Verona*, I, ii, 76–93, about the letter from Proteus:

Jul. Some love of yours hath writ to you in rhyme.
Luc. That I might *sing* it, madam, to a *tune*:
    Give me a note: your ladyship can *set*.
Jul. As little by such toys as may be possible:
    Best sing it to the tune of "Light o' love."
Luc. It is too heavy for so *light* a tune.
Jul. *Heavy?* belike, it hath some *burden* then.
Luc. Ay, and melodious were it, would you sing it.
Jul. And why not you?
Luc.   I cannot *reach so high*.
Jul. Let 's see your song.—How now, minion!
Luc. *Keep tune* there still, so you will *sing it out*;
    And yet, methinks, I do not like this tune.
Jul. You do not?
Luc.   No, madam, it is *too sharp*.
Jul. You, minion, are too saucy.
Luc.   Nay, now you are *too flat*,

And *mar the concord* with *too harsh a descant*:
There wanteth but a *mean* to fill your song.
Jul. The *mean* is *drown'd* with your *unruly base.*
Luc. Indeed, I bid the *base* for Proteus.

Perhaps it is sufficient to remark that many of the italicized words above are still in ordinary use by musicians—e.g. to "give the note" in order to "set" the pitch for singing; to "keep in tune," to "sing out"; or one voice is "drowned" by another, as the "mean" (alto) by the "base." Once more we have quibbles on musical terms—Lucetta says the "tune," i.e. Julia's testiness about Proteus's letter, is "too sharp," and that her chiding of herself is "too flat," meaning, that neither is in "concord" with the spirit of the love-letter. Lucetta recommends the middle course, or "mean" (alto voice, midway between treble and bass), "to *fill* the song," i.e. to perfect the harmony. Finally, there is a punning reference (somewhat prophetic) by Lucetta, to the "base" conduct of Proteus, in forsaking Julia for Silvia. Another play upon words should not be missed, viz. in lines 78 and 79, where "set" does double duty.

Romeo and Juliet, III, v, 25. Romeo and Juliet's parting at daybreak. The lark's song suggests musical metaphors in Juliet's speech.

Romeo. How is 't, my soul? let 's talk, it is not day.
Juliet. It is, it is; hie hence, be gone, away!
It is the *lark* that sings so *out of tune*,

Straining *harsh discords*, and unpleasing *sharps*.
Some say, the lark makes *sweet division*;
This doth not so, for she *divideth us.*

Juliet evidently agrees with Portia that "nothing
is good without respect." The lark heralds the dawn,
so Romeo must leave her, *ergo*, the lark sings "out
of tune," his strains are full of "discords" and
"sharps." The last two lines contain an interesting
allusion in the word "division," besides the pun on
"she *divideth us.*"

"Division" means, roughly, a brilliant passage, of
short notes, which is founded essentially on a much
simpler passage of longer notes. A cant term for the
old-fashioned variation (e.g. the variations of the *Har-
monious Blacksmith*) was "note-splitting," which at
once explains itself, and the older word "division."
A very clear example of divisions may be found in
"Rejoice greatly" in the *Messiah*. The long "runs"
on the second syllable of "Rejoice," consisting of
several groups of four semiquavers, are simply "divisions" or "note-splittings" of the first note of each
group.

The word, however, has a further use, namely, to
play "divisions" on a viol-da-gamba. This was a
favourite accomplishment of gentlemen in the sixteenth and seventeenth centuries. Sir Andrew Ague-
cheek numbered this amongst his attainments (see
Twelfth Night, I, iii, 24); and readers of *John Inglesant*

VIOL-DA-GAMBA (1611)   (*See page* 28)

(*From Canon Galpin's "Old English Instruments of Music"*)

Made by a man who might have known Shakespeare, viz. Henrie Jaye
of Southwark

ORGANS   (*See page* 30)

(From Canon Galpin's "Old English Instruments of Music")

(1) The little organ was hung on the player's shoulder by the strap, and was played with one hand, the other blew the bellows. (2) The larger instrument is a "positive," i e. not to be moved about, and requires a blower, see handle on left.

will remember that "Mr. Inglesant, being pressed to oblige the company, played a descant upon a ground bass in the Italian manner." Playing a descant on a ground bass meant playing extempore "divisions" or variations, to the harmony of a "ground bass" which (with its proper chords) was repeated again and again by the harpsichordist, until the viol player had exhausted his capacity to produce further "breakings" of the harmony.

In 1659 there was published an instruction book in this art, called *Chelys Minuritionum*, i.e. the "Tortoise-shell of Diminutions," hence (*chelys* meaning a lyre made of a tortoise-shell) "The Division Viol." The book is by Christopher Sympson, a Royalist soldier, who was a well-known viol-da-gamba player. The work is in three parts, the third of which is devoted to the method of ordering division on a ground.

To give his own words:

"Diminution or division to a ground, is the breaking either of the bass or of any higher part that is applicable thereto. The manner of expressing it is thus:

"A ground, subject, or bass, call it what you please, is prick'd down in two several papers; one for him who is to play the ground upon an organ, harpsichord, or what other instrument may be apt for that purpose; the other for him that plays upon the viol, who having the said ground before his eyes as his theme or subject, plays such variety of descant or division in concordance thereto as his skill and present invention do then suggest unto him."

(See the Appendix for an example by Sympson.)

Farther on, he distinguishes between "breaking the notes of the *ground*" and "descanting upon" the ground.

This phrase, "breaking" notes, may be taken as a partial explanation of several passages in Shakespeare, where "broken music" is referred to, although it has been conjectured that a better account of this may be found in the natural imperfection of the lute, which, being a *pizzicato* instrument (i.e. the strings were plucked, not played with a bow), could not do more than indicate the harmony in "broken" pieces, first a bass note, then perhaps two notes at once, higher up in the scale, the player relying on the hearer to piece the harmony together.

The correct explanation is that of Mr. Chappell (in Aldis Wright's Clarendon Press edition of *Henry V*), viz. that when a "consort" of viols was imperfect, i.e. if one of the players was absent, and an instrument of another kind, e.g. a flute, was substituted, the music was thus said to be "broken." Cf. Matthew Locke's *Compositions for Broken and Whole Consorts*, 1672.

Mr. Aldis Wright has given me references to Bacon's *Sylva Sylvarum*, iii, 278, and *Essay of Masque and Triumph,* which show that "broken music" was understood to mean *any combination of instruments of different kinds.*[1] In *Sylva Sylvarum* Bacon mentions several "consorts of Instruments" which agree well together; e.g. "the Irish Harp and Base-Viol agree well: the Recorder and Stringed Music agree well: Organs and the Voice agree well, etc. But the Virginals and the Lute . . . agree not so well." All these, and similar combinations, seem to have been described as "broken music."

In point, see *Henry V*, V, ii, 248, where Henry proposes to Katherine:

> *King Henry.* Come, your answer in *broken music;* for thy *voice is music,* and thy *English broken;* therefore, queen of all, Katherine, *break* they mind to me in *broken* English: Wilt thou have me?

Also see *Troilus and Cressida,* III, i, 52 ff. (quoted farther on).

An entirely separate use of "break" is in the phrase "broken time," which has the simple and obvious meaning that the notes do not receive their due length and proportion. In this connection we will take the passage of King Richard's speech in prison at Pontefract—when he hears music without, performed by some friendly hands.

[1] Bacon's *Essay on Masque and Triumph* speaks of "some good broken music," as the proper accompaniment to a masque ball. He means precisely, a "band."

Richard II, V, v, 41.   King Richard in prison.

> King Richard.   *Music* do I hear?
> Ha, ha! *keep time.*—How sour sweet music is,
> When *time is broke*, and no *proportion kept*!
> So is it in the music of men's lives.
> And here have I the *daintiness of ear*,
> To check *time broke* in a *disorder'd string*;
> But, for the *concord* of *my* state and *time*,
> Had not an *ear* to hear my true *time broke*.
>
> .   .   .   .   .
>
> *This music mads me:* let it sound no more:
> For though *it hath holp madmen* to their wits,
> In me, it seems, it will make wise men mad.

The simile is perfect, and the play upon "time broke" admirable.   In line 45 Richard reflects on the sad contrast between his quick "ear" for "broken time" in music, and his slowness to hear the "breaking" of his *own* "state and time."   The "disorder'd string" is himself, who has been playing his part "out of time" ("disorder'd" simply means "out of its place"—i.e. as we now say, "a bar wrong"), and this has resulted in breaking the "concord"—i.e. the harmony of the various parts which compose the state.

A few words are necessary about "proportion." This term was used in Elizabethan times exactly as we now use "time." [1]   The "times" used in modern music can practically be reduced to two—viz., duple

---

[1] Modern "time" is rather a matter of accent; the ancient "proportion" was more concerned with relative *lengths* of notes.

(two beats to the bar) and triple (three beats to the bar). But in Elizabeth's day the table of various proportions was a terribly elaborate thing. Of course, many of these "proportions" never really came into practical use—but there was plenty of mystery left even after all deductions.

Morley (*Introduction*, 1597) gives five kinds of proportions "in most common use" — viz., Dupla, Tripla, Quadrupla, Sesquialtera, and Sesquitertia. The first three correspond to what we still call duple, triple, and quadruple time—i.e. 2 in the bar, 3 in the bar, and 4 in the bar. ("Bars" were not in general use till the end of the sixteenth century,[1] but the principle was the same. The bars themselves are merely a convenience.)

Sesquialtera is more complicated, and means "three notes are sung to two of the same kinde"; and "Sesquitertia is when four notes are sung to three of the same kinde." "But," Morley adds, "if a man would ingulphe himselfe to learn to sing, and set down all them which Franchinus Gaufurius [1496] hath set down in his booke *De Proportionibus Musicis*, he should find it a matter not only hard but almost impossible."

Ornithoparcus,[2] in his *Micrologus* (1517), gives us

---

[1] But it was quite common to have no bars up to the middle of the seventeenth century.

[2] Ornithoparcus, real name Vogelsang, a native of Meiningen. His book was published in English by John Dowland, 1609.

an idea of the way this subject of proportion was treated by more "learned" writers. He says (1) that music considers only the proportion of inequality, (2) that this is twofold — viz., the greater and the lesser inequality. (3) The greater inequality contains five proportions, namely, multiplex, superparticular, superpartiens, multiplex superparticular, and multiplex superpartiens.

This is more amusing than instructive, perhaps. The three last lines of this passage refer to the various stories of real or pretended cure of disease by the use of particular pieces of music. One of the best-known of these diseases is "Tarantism,"[1] or the frenzy produced by the bite of the tarantula, in Italy.

Kircher, a learned Jesuit (1601–80), gives an account, in his *Musurgia*, of the cure of this madness by certain airs, by which the patient is stimulated to dance violently. The perspiration thus produced was said to effect a cure. In his *Phonurgia nova* (1673) Kircher actually gives the notes of the tune by which one case was cured.

[1] The late Sir Arthur Shipley, a distinguished zoologist, sent an interesting letter on Tarantism to *The Times*, 19 December, 1908. He recalls the seizures, "chiefly confined to the female sex," which spread all over Europe in the Middle Ages. St. Vitus's dance, and the Tarantella mania, were two of these. Paracelsus speaks of "treatment" for such disorders, e.g. solitary confinement, and discomfort, immersion in cold water, and so on. Tarantism was at its height in the seventeenth century, but St. Vitus's dance had long disappeared from Northern Europe.

In this connection, Kircher mentions King Saul's madness, which was relieved by David's harp playing. This is certainly to the point, and may well have been in Shakespeare's mind.

See also George Herbert's poem, *Doomsday*, verse 2:

> Dust, alas! no music feels
> But thy trumpet: then it kneels,
> As peculiar notes and strains
> Cure Tarantula's raging pains.

Our modern tarantellas derive their name and characteristic speed from the old tarantula.

King Lear, I, ii, 137. Edmund pretends not to see Edgar's entrance.

Edmund. [*Aside.*] Pat he comes, like the catastrophe of the old comedy: my cue is villainous melancholy, with a *sigh like Tom o' Bedlam.*—O! these eclipses do portend *these divisions. Fa, sol, la, mi.*

Songs like "Tom o' Bedlam," mad-songs they were called, were very commonly sung in England in the seventeenth century. The tune and words of the original "Tom o' Bedlam" are to be found in Chappell, vol. i, p. 175. Its date is some time before 1626,[1] and verse 1 begins, "From the hagg and hungrie Goblin." The last sentence has yet another play on the

[1] Rimbault's preface to the Musical Antiquarian Society's reprint of Purcell's opera, *Bonduca*, says that "Mad Tom" was written by Coperario in 1612, for the *Masque of the Inner Temple and Gray's Inn*, by Beaumont. This was, "Forth from my sad and darksome sell."

double meaning of "divisions." A few lines further on Edmund explains what kind of "divisions" he expects to follow the eclipses—namely, "between the child and the parent . . . dissolutions of ancient amities; divisions in state," etc. But the very use of the word in the quoted lines brings its musical meaning into his head, for he promptly carries off his assumed blindness to Edgar's presence by humming over his "Fa, sol, la, mi." [Burney, *History of Music*, vol. iii, p. 344, has a sensible observation on this passage—that Edgar alludes to the unnatural division of parent and child, etc., in this musical phrase, which contains the augmented fourth, or *Mi contra Fa*, of which the old theorists used to say, "diabolus est."]

Guido d'Arezzo (or Aretinus), in his *Micrologus* (about 1024), named the six notes of the Hexachord (e.g. C, D, E, F, G, A) thus: Ut, Re, Mi, Fa, Sol, La. These were the first syllables of certain words in the Hymn for the Feast of St. John Baptist, the words and tune of which are in Hawkins, p. 163:

> Ut queant laxis
> Re-sonare fibris
> Mi-ra gestorum
> Fa-muli tuorum
> Sol-ve polluti
> La-bii reatum, Sancte Joannes.[1]

[1] These syllables now appear to be of Arabian origin, adapted by Guido. See various works by H. G. Farmer.

A rough translation of which is:

That thy servants may be able with free hearts to sound forth the wonders of thy deeds; release us, O Holy John, from the guilt of a defiled lip.

In the ancient tune of this verse, the notes assigned to the syllables in capitals were successively those of the scale, C, D, E, F, G, A, and these same syllables were still used in singing in the sixteenth century. It was noticed, however, that the scale could be easily expressed by fewer names, and accordingly we find Christopher Sympson (1667) saying, in his *Compendium*, that Ut and Re are "superfluous, and therefore laid aside by most Modern Teachers." In his book, the whole scale of *eight* notes is named thus: Fa, Sol, La, Fa, Sol, La, *Mi*, Fa.[1] A modern Tonic Sol-faist would understand this arrangement quite differently. C, D, E would be called Do (instead of Ut), Re, Mi; then would follow F, G, A, under the names Fa, Sol, La; and the "leading note" (top note but one) would be called Ti (instead of Si); the octave C beginning once more with Do.

The reader will remember that the tonal relation of C, D, E, is exactly the same as that of the next three notes, F, G, A—viz., C—D, a tone; D—E, a tone; and similarly with F—G, G—A. Therefore the two blocks of three notes (which are separated by a *semi*-tone) might have the same names—viz., Fa,

[1] This is "Lancashire Sol-fa," in use quite recently in the North.

Sol, La. Thus we have the first *six* notes of the scale, Fa, Sol, La, Fa, Sol, La. There only remains one note, the "leading note," the B; and this, in Sympson, is named *Mi*. So the principal thing in the sol-faing of a passage was to "place the Mi," or, as we should now put it, to find "what key" it is in. Thus, in the key of C, Mi is B; in G, Mi is F sharp: in F, Mi is E, and so on, the remaining six notes being named Fa, Sol, La, Fa, Sol, La, as explained above.

Edmund's "Fa, sol, la, mi," therefore, corresponds to F, G, A, B; or C, D, E, F sharp; or B flat, C, D, E, etc.; according to the pitch taken by the singer.

In this connection see the following passage. *Taming of the Shrew*, I, ii, 16:

Petruchio.   Faith, sirrah, an you 'll not knock, I 'll *wring* it:
    I 'll try how you can *sol, fa*, and *sing it*.
                            [*He wrings Grumio by the ears.*

Here is a pun on "wring" and "ring"; and "sol, fa" is used as an equivalent for "sing."

More important still is "the gamut of Hortensio," III, i, 72. (Gam-ut was the name of the Ut of lowest pitch, corresponding to the low G on the first line of our present bass staff, and was marked specially with a Greek Gamma, hence Gam-ut. The word became a synonym for "the scale.")

In this passage the names of the notes are simply those to be found in all instruction books of the sixteenth and seventeenth centuries.

> Gam-ut I am, the ground of all accord,
> A-re, to plead Hortensio's passion;
> B-mi, Bianca, take him for thy lord,
> C-fa-ut, that loves with all affection:
> D-sol-re, one cliff, two notes have I:
> E-la-mi, show pity or I die.

Here Hortensio puts in his love-verses under the guise of a music-master's Gamut.

The lines may be taken separately as fantastic commentaries on the syllables themselves, as well as having their ulterior meaning for Bianca.

For instance, Gam-ut, the *lowest* note then recognised in the scale, is called "the *ground* of all *accord*." A-re, I suppose, represents the lover's sigh "to plead his passion." B-mi, may be twisted into "Be mine," by the light of the remaining words in the line; while "D-sol-re, one cliff, two notes have I" obviously refers to Hortensio's disguise. The "cliff" is what is now called a "clef," or "key," because its position on the staff gave the "key" to the position of the semitones and tones on the various lines and spaces. The six notes here mentioned are the G, A, B, C, D, E, in the bass staff. They could only be written (as they are yet) in *one* clef—namely, the F clef. The expression "two notes have I," as applied to the D, means that, in the key of G, D is called Sol; while in the key of C it would have the name Re; just as Hortensio is Hortensio, and at the same time masquerades as a singing-master.

It has been mentioned that the art of adding an extempore counterpoint to a written melody was called "descant." The written melody itself was called the "plain-song," and hence the whole performance, plain-song and descant together, came to be known by the term "plain-song," as opposed to the performance of plain-song with a *written* descant; which was known as "prick-song."

Morley gives us a clear idea that the extempore descant was often a very unsatisfactory performance, at any rate when it was attempted to add more than one extempore part at a time to the plain-song.   As he says: "For though they should all be moste excellent men . . . it is unpossible for them to be true one to another."   The following passage will be more clear in this light.

Henry V, III, ii, 3.   Fight at Harfleur.

Nym. Pray thee, corporal, stay: . . . the humour of it is too hot, that is the very *plain-song* of it.
Pistol. The plain-song is most just, for humours do abound.

Line 41:

Boy [*of the three rogues*]. . . . They will steal anything, and call it purchase.   Bardolph *stole a lute-case*, bore it twelve leagues, and *sold it for three half-pence.*

Falstaff's worthy body-guard are getting tired of hard knocks in fight; Nym compares their late activity to a somewhat florid "plain-song" (meaning an extempore descant, as explained above); Pistol says it is a "just" plain-song. A "just" plain-song would mean that the singer had managed his extempore descant "without singing eyther false chords or forbidden descant one to another." Similarly, there is little doubt that both Ancient and Corporal managed to take a part in the skirmishings with as little damage as possible to their sconces.

The speech of the boy at line 41 hardly enrols Bardolph amongst music lovers. At all events he stole a lute-case, and seems to have liked it so much that he carried it thirty-six miles before his worser nature prevailed on him to sell it for three halfpence.

The next quotation still concerns Jack Falstaff and his crew, all of whom (and strictly in accordance with history) seem to have been sound practical musicians. This time they are speaking, not of descant, but of prick-song. The chiefest virtue in the performance of prick-song, by which Falstaff and Nym probably understood both sacred and secular part-music, is that a man should "keep time," religiously counting his rests, "one, two, and the third in your bosom," and when he begins to sing, that he should "keep time, distance, and proportion," as Mercutio says

Tybalt did in his fencing; see *Romeo and Juliet*, II, iv, 20.

All this is thoroughly appreciated by Falstaff and his corporal in the following lines.

Merry Wives of Windsor, I, iii, 25:

> *Falstaff* [*of Bardolph*]. . . . his thefts were too open: his filching was *like an unskilful singer*, he *kept not time*.
> *Nym.* The good humour is to *steal at a minim's rest*.
> ["Minim's" is a modern conjecture.]

The metaphor is of an anthem or madrigal, say in four parts. We will suppose the Hostess of the "Garter" is taking the *Cantus*, a tapster the *Altus*, mine Host the *Tenor*, and Nym the *Bassus*. The three former are all hard at work on their respective "parts," one in the kitchen, another in the taproom, the third in familiar converse outside the front door. But Nym has "a minim rest," and during that short respite takes advantage of the absorbing occupations of the other three "singers" to lay hands on whatever portable property is within his reach. "A minim rest" is not much—but the point remains. Any musician has had experience of what can be done during a short "rest"—e.g. to resin his bow, or turn up the corners of the next few pages of his music, light the gas, or find his place in another book.

By an easy transition we pass to the following:

Pericles, I, i, 81. Pericles addresses the daughter of King Antiochus.

Per. You 're a *fair viol,* and *your sense the strings,*
   Who, *finger'd* to make man his *lawful music,*
   Would draw heaven down and all the gods to hearken;
   But being *play'd upon before your time,*
   Hell only danceth at so harsh a chime.

Pericles compares the lawful love of a wife with the performance of a good viol player, the proper characteristics of which would be, "in tune," and "in time." The comparison in line 84 is of this girl's lawless passion with the "disorder'd" playing of a bad violist, who has got "out," as we say; who is playing "before his time," thus entirely spoiling the music, which becomes a dance for devils rather than angels.

The viol was decidedly the most important stringed instrument played with a bow that was in use in Elizabethan times. There were three different sizes.

The reader will get a sufficiently accurate idea, both of the sizes and the use of viols, if he will consider the treble viol to have corresponded closely with our modern violin, the tenor viol to the modern viola (which is also called alto, tenor, or *Bratsche*— i.e. *braccio*, "arm" fiddle), and the bass viol, or viol-da-gamba (so called because held between the knees), to the modern violoncello.

The principal difference from our modern stringed instruments was that all the viols had *six* strings, whereas now there is no "fiddle" of any sort with more than four. A secondary difference was, that all the viol family had *frets* on the finger-board to mark out the notes, whereas the finger-boards of all our modern instruments are smooth, and the finger of the performer has to do without any help of that kind.[1]

John Playford, in 1683, published his *Introduction to the Skill of Music*, which gives an account of the viols; and Thomas Mace, of Cambridge, lay clerk of Trinity, in his *Musick's Monument*, published in 1676, gives full instructions how many viols and other instruments of this kind are necessary. From these we learn that viols were always kept in sets of six—two trebles, two tenors, and two basses—which set was technically known as a "chest" of viols. Mace also says that the treble viol had its strings just half the length of the bass viol, and the tenor was of a medium size between these. Also he says that if you add to these a couple of violins (which were then thought somewhat vulgar, loud instruments) for jovial occasions, and a pair of "lusty, full-sized theorboes," [2] "you have a ready entertainment for the greatest prince in the world."

The tuning of the six strings on the *bass* viol was:

[1] See Frontispiece.
[2] Theorbo, a lute with a double neck; so called from *tiorba*, a mortar for pounding perfumes, referring to the basin-shaped back of a lute.

on the bass staff, first string, or treble, D over the staff; second or small mean, A on the top line; third or great mean, E in the third space; fourth or counter-tenor, C in the second space; fifth or tenor, or gamut, G on the first line; and the sixth or bass, low D, under the staff. On the most complete viol there would be seven frets, arranged semitonally, so the compass of the bass viol or viol-da-gamba would be about two octaves and a half, from D under the bass staff to A on the second space of the treble staff. (In South Kensington Museum is a viol-da-gamba with no less than twelve frets still remaining. This would make the compass *three* octaves.)

The tenor viol had its top string tuned to G on the second line of the treble staff; and the remaining five were the same in pitch as the top five on the bass viol. The treble viol (as mentioned above) was tuned exactly an octave above the bass.

The tone of the viols is very much like that of our modern bowed instruments, the principal difference being that they are a little feebler, and naturally more calm. The reason is that vigorous "bowing" is a risky thing on the viol, for, as there are *six* strings on the arc of the bridge, more care is required to avoid striking two or even three at once than on the violin, which has only four.

The amateur of music would keep a "chest" of

six viols in his house, and when his musical friends visited him, they would generally play "Fancies" or Fantasias (see 2 *Henry IV*, III, ii, 323) in several parts, from two to the full six, according to the number of those present. Amongst a great number of composers of this kind of music, some very well-known names are, John Jenkins, Christopher Sympson, William Lawes, Coperario (John Cooper), and the Italian Monteverde. It was common for the organ or other keyed instrument to join with the viols in these pieces, and thus fill out the chords of the "consort," as it was called.

We still have one of the viol tribe left in our orchestra. The double-bass (or violone) is a lineal descendant of the chest of viols. Its shape, especially at the shoulders, is quite characteristic, and elsewhere—e.g. the blunt curves of the waist, the outline of the back, and even the shape of the bow.[1]

The practice of playing extempore variations on the viol-da-gamba has already been mentioned as one of the elegant accomplishments of a gentleman in those days. The following two quotations therefore will not require further remark.

[1] Since this was written, changes have taken place. The shape of the double-bass approximates to that of the violin; and the old curved bow has been given up in favour of a sturdy version of the violoncello bow. The old double-bass bow was held with the thumb over the nut, and this was also the case with the viol-da-gamba.

Twelfth Night, I, iii, 24:

Maria [of Sir Andrew Aguecheek]. . . . he's a very fool, and a prodigal.
Sir Toby. Fie, that you'll say so! he *plays o' the viol-de-gamboys* . . . and hath all the good gifts of nature.

Richard II, I, iii, 159.   Banishment of Norfolk.

Norfolk. The language I have learn'd these forty years,
   My native English, now I must forgo;
   And now my tongue's use is to me no more
   Than an *unstringed viol,* or a *harp;*
   Or like a *cunning instrument cas'd up,*
   Or, being open, *put into his hands*
   That knows *no touch to tune the harmony.*

The *violin* family had only a precarious footing amongst musicians up to 1650.   After that time, the viols declined in favour, and so rapidly, that at the very beginning of the eighteenth century, Dr. Tudway of Cambridge describes a chest of viols, in a letter to his son, with such particularity, that it is clear they had entirely fallen out of use by 1700.[1]   As the viol fell out of fashion, the violin took its place, and has kept it ever since.

The violin family had come into general and fashionable use under the patronage of the Court of Louis XIV, and thus the English nation, true to their

[1] With the exception of the viol-da-gamba, which was still being played, and written for, in Bach's time.

ancient habit of buying their "doublet in Italy, round hose in France, bonnet in Germany, and behaviour everywhere," took up the "French fiddles," and let their national chest of viols go to the wall.

This growing tendency to adopt French customs, even in music, is referred to in the following:

Henry VIII, I, iii, 41.   French manners in England.

Lovell. A French song, and a *fiddle*, has no fellow.
Sands. The devil fiddle 'em! I am glad they're going;
   For, sure, there's no converting of 'em: *now*,
   An honest country lord, as I am, beaten
   A long time out of *play*, may bring his *plain-song*,
   And have an hour of hearing: and, by 'r lady,
   Held *current music* too.

The only word here that has not already been fully explained is "current music," which I suppose to mean simply, that the old accomplishments of which Lord Sands speaks would be still thought "up to date" and in the fashion.

Another instrument in common domestic use was the recorder. This was a kind of "beak-flute," like a flageolet, but instead of six holes, the recorder had eight, or nine (one of which was stopped with wax, being a duplicate for a left-handed player).[1]

The recorder was known for its sweet tone. Poets

---

[1] Cf. Rabelais, *Gargantua,* chap. xxiii, where we are told that Gargantua learned to play on the "flûte à neuf trous" (recorder) as well as on the "flûte d'alleman" (German or traverse flute).

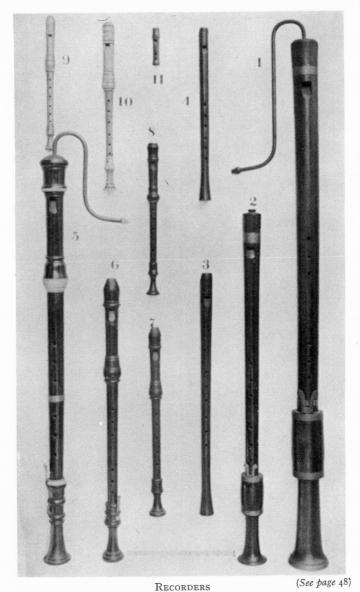

RECORDERS   *(See page* 48)

(From Canon Galpin's "Old English Instruments of Music")

Nos. 1–4 is a set, about 1600. Nos. 9 and 10 are of ivory. The short
pipe (No. 11) is a "picco," see p. 79.

VIRGINAL

(*From Canon Galpin's "Old English Instruments of Music"*)

Made by A. Rückers, 1610. The words on the lid are the last verse of Psalm cl. The tops of the "jacks" are seen under the rail. The low E was often tuned to C, the F♯ to D, and the G♯ to E. Peter Phillips shows this in his *Galiarda Dolorosa* (Fitzwilliam Book).

(*See page 52*)

used the word "record" to signify the song of birds, especially of the nightingale.[1]

Hawkins indentifies it with the "Fistula Dulcis, seu Anglica," and gives two pictures which help to explain the next quotation.

Hamlet, III, ii, 346. Enter Players with recorders.

Hamlet. O! the *recorders*: let me see one. . . .

.   .   .   .   .

Line 351.

Ham. . . . Will you *play upon this pipe?*
Guildenstern. My lord, I cannot.

.   .   .   .   .

Ham. 'Tis as easy as lying: govern these *ventages* with your *finger and thumb*, give it *breath* with your mouth, and it will discourse *most excellent music*. Look you, these are *the stops*.
Guil. But these cannot I command to any utterance of *harmony*: I have not the skill.
Ham. Why, look you now, how unworthy a thing you make of *me*. You would *play upon me*: you would seem to *know my stops*; . . . you would *sound me* from my *lowest note* to the *top of my compass*; and there is *much music*, excellent[2] voice, in *this little organ* [the recorder], yet cannot you make it *speak*. 'Sblood! do you think I am *easier to*

[1] Further information about recorders may be found in my *Poets and Music* (Dent), p. 94; and C. Welch's book on recorders (Frowde, 1911), especially p. 167, where a picture shows exactly what happens in *Hamlet*.
[2] This word "excellent" may be a pun. There is some evidence that the smallest size of recorder was called "exilent," from the Latin *exilis*, which means "thin."

be played on than a pipe? Call me what *instrument* you will, though you can *fret* me, you cannot *play* upon me.

The holes in a flute have always been called "ventages," because the "wind" comes through them when the fingers are removed. They were "governed" "with the finger and thumb." One of the illustrations from Mersennus (b. 1588) shows a conical flute with four holes in front and two at the back. These latter would, of course, be controlled by the *thumbs*, while the others would occupy two fingers on each hand. (Modern flageolets still keep a thumb-hole at the back.) There were other beaked flutes of the same period, of a better class, which had several keys as well as the holes.[1]

"The stops" referred to by Hamlet are merely the "ventages." The act of covering a hole with the finger or thumb was called "stopping"; and further, one example of the "fistula dulcis" given by Mersennus has two different holes for the lowest note, one on the right and the other on the left, so that the instrument might be used either by a right-handed or left-handed person. One of these two duplicate holes was temporarily *stopped* with wax. (The passing play upon "fret" in the last line should not be missed.)

In the next passage the meaning of "stop" as

[1] For the "eunuch" flute (the "pipe small as an eunuch" of *Coriolanus*, III, ii, 115), which was not a flute at all, but an instrument sung or hummed into by the performer, see my *Poets and Music*, p. 97.

applied to recorders is punned on by Hippolyta, who carries on the play from Lysander's horsebreaking metaphor.

Midsummer Night's Dream, V, i, 108. The Prologue speaks with all the punctuation wrong.

Theseus. This fellow doth not *stand upon points*.
Lysander. He hath rid his prologue like a rough colt; he knows not the *stop*. . . .
Hippolyta. Indeed, he hath played on this prologue like a *child on a recorder, a sound,* but *not in government.*

That is, the Prologue has misplaced all his *stops* —like a young horse that refuses to *stop*—also like a child who has not learned to *stop* the holes on the flute *à bec*.

It is singular that the virginal, which was the most popular of all the keyed instruments, is nowhere directly named in Shakespeare. There is, however, a reference to the action of the fingers on its keys in the following.

Winter's Tale, I, ii, 125. Of Hermione, Queen of Leontes, King of Sicilia, and Polixenes, King of Bohemia.

> *Leon*. . . . Still *virginalling*
> Upon his palm?

The virginal (generally known as "a *pair* of virginals") was most commonly used by ladies for their private recreation, and from this circumstance is supposed to derive its name. Queen Elizabeth

was fond of playing on it, but as it was in vogue
before her time, there is no need to connect the
name with the Virgin Queen. (Elizabeth's own
virginal is in South Kensington Museum.[1]) Its key-
board had four octaves, and the case was square,[2]
like that of a very old pianoforte. The strings of
the virginal were plucked, by quills,[3] which were
secured to the "jacks" (see *Sonnet CXXVIII*),[4] which
in turn were set in motion by the keys. The strings
were wire. The oldest country dance known, the
"Sellenger's [St. Leger's] Round," of Henry VIII's
time, was arranged by Byrd as a virginal "lesson"
for "Lady Nevell's booke." Another well-known
virginal book, that at the Fitzwilliam Museum at
Cambridge, commonly known as *Queen Elizabeth's
Virginal Book*, has been published by Breitkopf and
Härtel (1899).

The first music ever printed for the virginals was
Parthenia, published in London, 1611.[5] This collection contains principally pavans and galliards by

[1] See Frontispiece.

[2] Mr. A. J. Hipkins told me that the case was not necessarily
square.

[3] Plectra of leather were also in use, as well as those of quill.

[4] The true explanation of *Sonnet CXXVIII* is given in my book,
Poets and Music (Dent), pp, 91, 92, with two pictures of a lady doing
what the sonnet describes. The explanation was first published in
1910, in the April issue of the *Musical Antiquary* (Frowde).

[5] Music was first printed from copper-plates in Rome, in 1586.
See William Gamble's *Music Engraving* (Pitman, 1923), p. 49.

Byrd, Bull, and Gibbons. The title "Parthenia, or the Maydenhead of the firste musicke," etc., with a picture of a young lady playing on the virginal, seems to confirm our explanation of the name of this instrument.

Next to the viol, the lute [1] was the most popular stringed instrument. It was used both as a solo instrument on which to play sprightly "ayres," or as an accompaniment for the voice, or "in consort" with other instruments. Naturally, it figured frequently in "serenading" especially when a love song had to be sung outside a lady's window. The general shape of a lute is that of a mandoline, but about four times as big. Like the mandoline, it has a flat belly, and a great basin-shaped back. But in every other respect it is entirely different. It is used more in the fashion of a guitar, and its strings (which should be of gut) are plucked with the fingers.

Adrian Le Roy's book, published in Paris about 1570, says the six strings were tuned as follows: first (minikin), C in third space, treble staff; second (small mean), G on second line; third (great mean), D under the staff; fourth (counter-tenor), B flat over the bass staff; fifth (tenor), F on fourth line; and sixth (base), C in second space.

Scipione Cerreto, however (Naples, 1601), gives quite a different account of the Italian lute of eight

[1] See Frontispiece.

strings, the tuning of which seems to have extended the compass downwards to C under the bass staff. Thomas Mace (*Musick's Monument*, 1676) tells of several objections against the lute, the most note-worthy of which were: first, that it was a costly instrument to keep in repair; second, that it was out of fashion; and third, that it *made young people grow awry*. Mace refutes these calumnies, the last of which no doubt was set about on account of the very awkward shape of the lute-back, and the considerable size of the instrument. Hawkins (*History of Music*, pp. 730 and 731) gives two pieces for the lute by Mace, or, rather, the same piece twice, first for one lute, then arranged for two. (See Appendix.)

The five lower strings of the lute were "doubled"— i.e. there were two of each pitch, duplicates, which helped the tone of the chords by "sympathetic" vibration. So there were really eleven strings, but only six different pitches. There were eight frets on the finger-board.

Other varieties were the arch-lute [1] and the theorbo-lute, both of which had very long double necks, and a large number of strings. One arch-lute in South Kensington Museum has as many as twenty-four, eleven of which are duplications. [2]

[1] See Frontispiece.

[2] See my *Poets and Music* (Dent), p. 109 ff, for the important explanation of *Sonnet VIII*, which depends entirely on the fact that the strings were tuned in pairs, except the highest, which was single.

1 *Henry VI*, I, iv, 92:

Talbot [*of Salisbury dying*].
  He beckons with his hand, and smiles on me,
  As who should say, "When I am dead and gone,
  Remember to avenge me on the French."—
  Platagenet, I will; and *like thee*, *Nero*,
  Play on the lute, beholding the towns burn.

   1 *Henry IV*, III, i, 206, Mortimer to Lady Mortimer.

Mort.   . . . for thy tongue
  Makes Welsh as sweet as *ditties* highly penn'd,
  Sung by a fair queen in a summer's bower,
  With *ravishing division*, to her *lute*.

For "ravishing division," see the remarks on the third of the foregoing passages, the speech of Juliet about the lark's song (p. 28).

The lute leads us quite easily from Musical Instruments and Technical Terms to the second division.

II

THE following passages give a lively picture of what a music-master might have to put up with from young ladies of quality.

Taming of the Shrew, II, i, 142. Re-enter Hortensio with his head broken.

Bap. How now, my friend? why dost thou look so pale?
Hor. For fear, I promise you, if I look pale.
Bap. What, will my daughter [Kate] prove a good musician?
Hor. I think, she'll sooner prove a soldier:
   Iron may hold with her, but never *lutes*.
Bap. Why, then thou canst not *break her* to the lute?
Hor. Why, no, for *she hath broke the lute to me*.
   I did but tell her she *mistook her frets*,
   And bow'd her hand to *teach her fingering*,
   When, with a most impatient, devilish spirit,
   "*Frets* call you these?" quoth she; "I 'll *fume* with them";
   And with that word she struck me on the head,
   And *through the instrument my pate made way*;
   And there I stood amazed for a while,
   As on a pillory, looking through the lute,
   While she did call me *rascal fiddler*,
   And *twangling Jack*, with twenty such vile terms,
   As she had studied to misuse me so.

Line 277:

Bap. Why, how now, daughter Katherine? in your *dumps*?

Again, III, i. Hortensio and Lucentio, the sham musical and classical tutors, give a lesson to Bianca. They quarrel which is to start first.

Lucentio. Fiddler, forbear : you grow too forward, sir.

.   .   .   .   .

Hortensio. But, wrangling pedant, *this is*
   The patroness of heavenly harmony;
   Then give me leave to have prerogative,
   And *when in music we have spent an hour,*
   Your lecture shall have leisure for as much.
Luc. Preposterous ass,[1] that never read so far
   To know the cause why music was ordained!
   Was it not to refresh the mind of man,
   After his studies, or his usual pain?
   Then give me leave to read philosophy,
   And *while I pause, serve in your harmony.*

Bianca settles the question, and orders Hortensio (line 22):

   Take you your instrument, *play you the whiles;*
   His lecture will be done, *ere you have tun'd.*
Hor. You'll leave his lecture, when I am in tune?
Luc. That will be never : tune your instrument.

Lucentio now goes on with his "classics"; farther on:

Hor. [*Returning.*] Madam, *my instrument's in tune.*
Bianca. Let's hear. [*Hor. plays.*] O fie! the *treble jars.*

---

[1] "Preposterous ass" reminds one of Thomas Morley's delightful words "To the Reader" of his *Plain and Easy Introduction to Practical Music* (1597): "And as for those ignorant Asses, who take upon them to lead others, none being more blind than themselves . . ."

Luc. Spit in the hole, man, and tune again.
.   .   .   .   .
Hor. Madam, 'tis now in tune.
Luc.   All but the *base*.
Hor. The base is right; 'tis the *base knave* that *jars*.

Hortensio now takes his place, and addresses the classical Lucentio.

Line 58:

Hor. You may go walk, and give me leave awhile:
My *lessons* make no music in *three parts*.
.   .   .   .   .

Line 63:

Hor. Madam, before you *touch* the instrument,
   To learn the *order of my fingering*,
   I must begin with *rudiments* of art;
   To teach you *gamut* in a briefer sort,
   More pleasant, pithy, and effectual
   Than hath been taught by any of my trade
   And there it is in writing, fairly drawn.
Bianca. Why, I am *past my gamut* long ago.
Hor. Yet read the gamut of Hortensio.

The first of these three passages will be quite clear to the reader in the light of the remarks on the lute already made. The second should be read in connection with the name of the doleful dance above mentioned, the dump. (See Appendix.)

The third quotation contains interesting allusions to the peculiarities of the lute. Lines 22–5 are very naturally accounted for. The lute, having at least

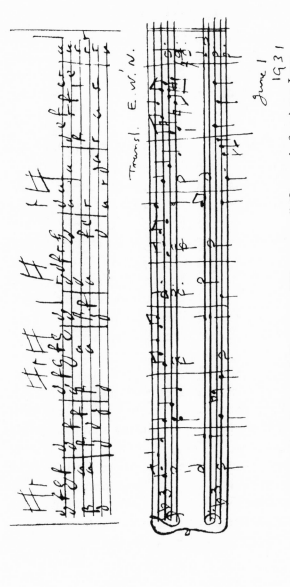

Transl. E. v. N.

June 1
1931

FIRST LINE OF DOWLAND'S SETTING OF "WALSINGHAM" (OPHELIA'S SONG) FOR LUTE

From Cambridge University Lute MS., Dd. 9, 33, fol. 67b. The setting has eighteen lines, and fills up two pages of the MS. The note "a" is missing from the melody at the first beat of bar 7.

eleven strings, took a long time to get into tune.
Even our modern violins, with only four strings, want
constant attention in this respect; and the lute,
therefore, especially in the hands of an amateur,
might well get a name for being a troublesome
instrument. The reference to the "treble" and
"bass" strings (i.e. the first and sixth) has been
explained before. "Spit in the hole, man," Lucentio's
advice to Hortensio, which sounds rude, but is merely
a practical way to stop the peg from slipping, may
direct our attention to the variously shaped "holes"
which were made in the belly of all stringed instruments to let out the sound. On the lute, this hole
was commonly a circular opening, not clearly cut
out, but fretted in a circle of small holes with a
star in the middle. But this was not the only way.
A lute in South Kensington Museum has *three* round
holes, placed in an oblique line, nearly at the bottom
of the instrument.[1] The holes on the viol were
generally in the form of crescents, and were put one
on each side of the bridge. On the modern violins, as
everybody has seen, they are in the shape of ʃ ʅ ,
and are known as "*f*" holes.

Line 59, about "lessons in three parts," is of
interest. Primarily, it is another form of "Two's
company, three is none"—but its musical meaning
is very plainly present. In the sixteenth and seven-

[1] See Frontispiece.

teenth centuries it was very common to call the pieces of music in any volume for an instrument by the name "lessons." The first meaning, of course, was that they were examples for the pupil in music, but the word was used quite freely with the purely general signification of "pieces" or "movements."

One more word deserves remark—viz., "to touch," in line 63. This is used technically, and means strictly "to play" on the instrument. The word is connected both in meaning and form with Italian *toccare*.

Toccata was a common word for a prelude (often extempore), intended as a kind of introduction to two or three more formal movements. The Italian for a peal of bells is *tocco di campana*, and we have the word in English under the form *tocsin*, an alarm bell. The trumpet-call known as "tucket," which occurs seven times in the stage directions of six Shakespeare plays, and is also found once in the text (*Henry V*, IV, ii, 35), is from the same root as *toccare*. Similarly with the German *Tusch*, a flourish of trumpets and other brass instruments, which may be heard under that name to the present day.

The next passage confirms Morley's account of the high estimation in which music was held as a part of a liberal education. Baptista evidently considers "good bringing up" to include "music, instruments, and poetry." Moreover, the visiting

master was to be well paid—"to cunning men I will
be very kind."

Taming of the Shrew, I, i, 81:

Bianca. Sir, to your pleasure humbly I subscribe:
 My books, and *instruments*, shall be my company,
 On them to look, and *practise by myself.*

.   .   .   .   .

Baptista. Go in, Bianca.   [*Exit Bianca.*
 And for I know, she taketh most delight
 In *music, instruments*, and *poetry*,
 Schoolmasters will I keep within my house,
 Fit to instruct her youth.—If you, Hortensio,
 Or Signior Gremio, you, know any such,
 Refer them hither; for *to cunning men
 I will be very kind*, and liberal
 To mine own children in *good bringing up.*

We find farther on, in the same play, that to bring
one's lady-love a music-master was thought a hand-
some compliment.

Ibid., I, ii, 170:

Hortensio. 'Tis well: and I have met a gentleman,
 Hath promis'd me to help me to another,
 A fine musician to instruct our mistress.

Moreover, in *Pericles*, IV, vi, 185, we find that
Marina, daughter of Prince Pericles, can "*sing*, weave,
sew, and *dance*." Also see V, i, 78, where Marina
actually does sing, to rouse her father from his
melancholy.

III

It is impossible here to give even an outline of the history of Songs and Singing in England. The general statement must suffice that vocal music, accompanied by viols and harps, with songs and catches, was common in the thirteenth century in France; and any reader of Chaucer and Gower may see for himself that vocal music was flourishing in the fourteenth century in England. The English round or catch, mentioned above, "Sumer is icumen in," is most probably of the thirteenth century, and that alone would be sufficient to characterize the popular vocal music of that day. This composition is advanced in every way, being very melodious, and at the same time showing that vocal harmony (i.e. singing in parts) was greatly appreciated.

To proceed to a time nearer the age with which we are concerned—in Henry VIII's reign, there were many songs written, some for voices only, and some with instrumental accompaniment. Amongst the former are two songs in three parts, the music by

William Cornysshe, Junior, which are given in Hawkins.[1]

Skelton wrote the words of the first, "Ah, beshrew you by my fay," which is very coarse in tone, as was frequently the case with him; and the second one, "Hoyday, jolly ruttekin," is a satire on the drunken habits of the Flemings who came over with Anne of Cleves. Mrs. Page (*Merry Wives of Windsor*, II, i, 23) refers to these Dutchmen, where, after receiving Falstaff's love-letter, she exclaims: "What an un-weighed behaviour hath this *Flemish drunkard* picked (with the devil's name!) out of my conversation, that he dares in this manner assay me?"

The following is a curious picture by "Skelton, Laureate," of an ignorant singer, who appears to have been throwing mud at the poet. Skelton gives us a sad account both of his morals and his music.

Beginning at the third verse:

> With hey troly loly, lo whip here Jak,
> Alumbek, sodyldym syllorym ben,
> Curiously he can both *counter* and knak,
> Of Martin Swart, and all his merry men;
> Lord, how Perkyn is proud of his Pohen,
> But ask wher he findeth among his *monachords*
> An holy-water-clark[2] a ruler of lordes.

---

[1] Other songs in three parts, by Cornysshe and King Henry VIII, are printed in my book, *Shakespeare Music* (Curwen), p. 63 ff.

[2] A holy water clerk was a humble servant of the Church, hence Skelton's scorn of such a one posing as "ruler of lordes." *Aquæ*

He cannot fynd *it* in *rule* nor in *space*,
He *solfyth* too haute, hys *trybyll* is too high,
He braggyth of his byrth that borne was full base,
Hys musyk *withoute measure, too sharp* is *his* 'my,'
He trymmeth in his *tenor* to *counter* pardy,
His *descant* is besy,[1] it is without a *mene*,
Too fat is his fantsy, his wyt is too lene.

He tumbryth on a *lewde lewte*, Rotybulle Joyse,
Rumbill downe, tumbill downe, hey go, now now,
He *fumblyth in his fyngering* an ugly rude noise,
It seemyth the sobbying of an old sow:
He wolde be made moch of, and he wyst how;
Well sped in spindels and tuning of travellys,
A bungler, a brawler, a picker of quarrellys.

Comely he clappyth a *payre of clavicordys*,
He *whystelyth* so swetly he maketh me to swet,
His *discant* is dashed full of *discordes*,
A red angry man, but easy to intrete; etc.

Farther on we read:

For lordes and ladyes lerne at his scole,
He techyth them so wysely to *solf* and to *fayne*,
That neither they sing wel *prike-song* nor *plain*.

Skelton's main objection to this person is that he,

bajulus was his Latin designation, as one of his duties was to asperse holy water at private houses on festivals.

He sometimes got an exhibition to the university, and so became a priest. Bequests from the Parochus to help the "clark" in this way are to be found in 1260 and 1337. See Serjeantson's *History of St. Giles, Northampton.*

[1] "Besy," that is, "busy," meaning "fussy," a bad fault in descant, as it is to-day in counterpoint.

being in reality of very humble origin, presumed on his very doubtful musical abilities to gain a footing amongst his betters.   As he says: "For Jak wold be a jentilman that late was a grome."

Evidently "Jak" had managed to make good his position as a fashionable teacher of singing, in spite of the defects plainly mentioned in the above verses. In the first verse, "counter" is a musical term, here used with the meaning of "to embroider" the tale. "Knack" is still used in Yorkshire for "affected talk." "Monachord" is the ancient one-stringed fiddle called tromba marina,[1] and is here used as a joke on "monachi" or "holy-water clarks."   In verse 2, "*rule* and space" is simply "line and space," i.e. on the music alstaff, "He cannot find it," *it* being the key-note.   "Solfyth too haute" is "Sol-fa's too high." The "my" which was "too sharp" is the Mi, the seventh note of the scale, mentioned above as the critical point in Sol-fa.   In verse 3, "lewde lewte" means   merely   "vulgar   lute";   and   "Rotybulle Joyse" is the title of an old song.   The "payre of clavicordys" is the clavichord, which in 1536 was a keyed instrument of much the same kind as the

---

[1] Or sea-trumpet. Monsieur Jourdain's favourite instrument: "La trompette marine est un instrument qui me plaît, et qui est harmonieux" (*Le Bourgeois Gentilhomme*, II, i). It is as tall as a man. Melodies can be played on it, by using the harmonics, as on the strings of a double-bass. It got the name "marine trumpet" from its shape, which was like an old-fashioned speaking-trumpet.

virginals,[1] with about three and a half octaves. It was used by nuns, and therefore had its strings muffled with bits of cloth to deaden the sound, so they used to say. As a matter of fact, these bits of cloth were for a much more important purpose, viz. to stop the portion of the string on the near side of the tangent from playing another note.

The last three lines quoted mention "sol-fa" and "fayne." The latter is "feigned" music, or "musica ficta," which at this time was the art of dislocating the "Mi," so as to change the key. It was seldom that more than one flat was found in those days, and this would move the Mi from B to E, thus constituting "fayned" music.

This account will give a general idea of the kind of songs and singing that were to be found in 1500.

Popular songs, "Rotybulle Joyse," with a burden of "Rumbill downe, tumbill downe," etc., accompanied by a "lewde lewte"; clavichord playing; sol-faing; singing of both "prick-" and "plain-" song, with "musica ficta"; besides the delectable art of "whysteling"; seem to have been matters in ordinary

[1] It was the *German* clavichord that had "tangents" of brass at the ends of the key levers. These tangents cut off the proper length of the string, and made it sound at the same time. The Italians called an instrument with a "jack" action like the virginal by the name clavichord.

N.B.—The clavichord was also named monachord or manichord. Skelton probably does not refer to the keyed instrument, for he mentions the "payre of clavicordys" farther on.

practice at the beginning of the sixteenth century. Add to these the songs in three parts, with rounds or catches for several voices, and we have no mean list of musicianly accomplishments which the men of Shakespeare's day might inherit.

In Shakespeare, besides the songs most commonly known (some of which are by earlier authors), there are allusions to many kinds of vocal music, and scraps of the actual words of old songs—some with accompaniment, some without; a duet; a trio; a chorus; not to mention several rounds, either quoted or alluded to.

It will be useful here to refer to a few of these less known examples.

Love's Labour 's Lost, I, ii, 106. The ballad of "The King and the Beggar." Moth says; "The world was very guilty of such a ballad some three ages since; but I think now 'tis not to be found; or, if it were, it would neither serve for the writing, nor the tune."

Ibid., III, i, 2. Moth begins a song, "Concolinel," which Armado calls a "sweet air."

Various snatches of ballads, ancient and modern —e.g.:

(*a*) By Falstaff, 2 *Henry IV*, II, iv, 32: "When Arthur first in court began, And was a worthy king."

(*b*) By Master Silence, 2 *Henry IV*, V, iii, 18: "Do

nothing but eat, and make good cheer," etc.; "Be merry, be merry, my wife has all," etc.; "A cup of wine, that 's brisk and fine," etc.; "Fill the cup, and let it come," etc.; "Do me right, And dub me knight," etc.; "And Robin Hood, Scarlet, and John."

(c) By Benedick, *Much Ado about Nothing*, V, ii, 23: "The god of love."

(d) The old tune "Light o' Love" (see Appendix), the original words of which are unknown. *Much Ado about Nothing*, III, iv, 41: "Clap us into 'Light o' love'; that goes without a burden; do you sing it, and I 'll dance it." Here is one verse of "A very proper Dittie," to the tune of "Lightie Love" (date 1570):

> By force I am fixed my fancie to write,
> Ingratitude willeth me not to refrain:
> Then blame me not, ladies, although I indite
> What lighty love now amongst you doth rayne,
> Your traces in places, with outward allurements,
> Dothe moove my endevour to be the more playne:
> Your nicyngs and tycings, with sundrie procurements,
> To publish your lightie love doth me constraine.

There were several songs of the sixteenth century that went to this tune. See also Shakespeare, *Two Gentlemen of Verona*, I, ii, 80, and Fletcher, *Two Noble Kinsmen*, V, ii, 54.

(e) Song by Parson Evans, *Merry Wives of Windsor*, III, i, 18: "To shallow rivers," for words of which see

Marlowe's "Come live with me," printed in the *Passionate Pilgrim* (see tunes in Appendix). Sir Hugh is in a state of nervous excitement, and the word "rivers" brings "Babylon" into his head, so he goes on mixing up a portion of the version of Ps. cxxxvii with Marlowe.

(*f*) By Sir Toby, *Twelfth Night*, II, iii, 79, 85, 102: "Peg-a-Ramsey," "Three merry men be we," "There dwelt a man in Babylon," "O! the twelfth day of December," "Farewell, dear heart."[1] (For tunes, see Appendix.)

(*g*) *As You Like It*, II, v: Song with chorus, "Under the greenwood tree"; second verse, "*All together here.*"

(*h*) By Pandarus, *Troilus and Cressida*, III, i, 116: Song, "Love, love, nothing but love," accompanied on an "instrument" by the singer himself.

(*i*) Another, ibid., IV, iv, 14: "O heart, heavy heart."

(*j*) *King Lear*, I, iv, 168: two verses sung by the Fool, "Fools had ne'er less grace in a year."

(*k*) Ballads by Autolycus, *Winter's Tale*, IV, ii, 1,

---

[1] "Farewell, dear heart," is an interesting case of a newly-published song being inserted in a new play. Robert Jones set it for lute with four voices in 1600. The date of *Twelfth Night* is 1601. For the original music and words, see my *Shakespeare Music* (Curwen), p. 22 and 23, which also shows how Sir Toby and the Clown would perform their tipsy version.

The tune was used as a hymn tune in 1713, and set to Dutch words beginning, "Heilgierig mensch, wiens grondgedachten t' Geniet van lust en rust betrachten."

15: "When daffodils"; "But shall I go mourn for that?" ibid., sc. ii, end: "Jog on" (see Appendix); ibid., sc. iii, 198: "Whoop, do me no harm, good man" (Appendix); ibid., l. 219: "Lawn, as white as driven snow"; ibid., l. 262: ballad of the "Usurer's wife," to a "very doleful tune"; ibid., l. 275: ballad of a Fish, "very pitiful"; ibid., l. 297: a song *in three parts*, to the tune of "Two maids wooing a man," "Get you hence, for I must go"; ibid., l. 319: song, "Will you buy any tape?" (cf. the round by Jenkins [b. 1592], "Come, pretty maidens," see Rimbault's *Rounds, Canons, and Catches*).

(*l*) Duet by King Cymbeline's two sons; funeral song over Imogen, *Cymbeline*, IV, ii, 258: "Fear no more the heat o' the sun."

(*m*) Stephano's "scurvy tunes," *Tempest*, II, ii, 41: "I shall no more to sea," "The master, the swabber," etc. (Appendix).   Ibid., l. 175: Caliban's song, "Farewell, master," etc.

(*n*) Song accompanied by lute, *Henry VIII*, III, i: "Orpheus." [1]

Besides these there are allusions to the names of various popular tunes and catches, of which the music is still to be had.   Amongst these are:

"The hunt is up" (Appendix).   See *Romeo and*

[1] See J. M. Gibbon's *Melody and the Lyric* (Dent, 1930), p. 108, for the song "King Stephen," or "Tak' thy auld cloak about thee," sung by Iago (*Othello*, II, iii), and referred to by Trinculo (*Tempest*, IV, i).

Juliet, III, v, 34. Juliet says of the lark's song: "That voice doth us affray, Hunting thee hence with *hunts-up* to the day." Any rousing morning song, even a love-song, was called a *hunts-up*. The tune of this song was also sung (in 1584) to "O sweete Olyver, leave me not behind the," but altering the time to four in a bar. See *As You Like It*, III, iii, 95.

"Heart's Ease" (Appendix), the words of which are not known. Tune before 1560. See *Romeo and Juliet*, IV, v, 100.

Ibid., "My heart is full of woe."

Ibid., l. 125: "When griping grief" (Appendix), by Richard Edwards, gentleman of Queen Elizabeth's Chapel, published in the *Paradyse of Daynty Devises* (printed 1577). Hawkins gives four verses, the first of which is here quoted by Shakespeare, but with several variations:

> *Where* griping grief the hart *would* wound,
> And doleful domps the mind oppresse,
> *There* Musick with her silver sound
> *Is wont with spede to give* redresse;
> Of troubled minds, for every sore,
> Swete Musick hath a salve in store.

The last verse is charming:

> Oh heavenly gift, that turnes the minde,
> Like as the sterne doth rule the ship,
> Of musick whom the Gods assignde,
> To comfort man whom cares would nip;
> Sith thou both man and beast doest move,
> What wise man then will thee reprove?

"Green Sleeves" (Appendix). *Merry Wives of Windsor*, II, i, 60:

> *Mrs. Ford.* . . . . I would have sworn his disposition [Falstaff's] would have gone to the truth of his words; but they do *no more adhere* and *keep place* together, than the *Hundredth Psalm* to the *tune of "Green Sleeves."*

And again, V, v, 20. The tune is given in its most complete form by Chappell, and is probably of Henry VIII's time. The ballad was published in 1580, with title, "A new Northerne dittye of the Ladye Greene Sleeves." Verse 1 is as follows:

> Alas, my love, you do me wrong
> To cast me off discourteously,
> And I have lovèd you so long,
> Delighting in your company.
> Greensleeves was all my joy,
> Greensleeves was my delight,
> Greensleeves was my heart of gold,
> And who but my Lady Greensleeves?

The Hundredth Psalm ("All people that on earth do dwell") will only adhere and keep place with the tune of "Green Sleeves" to a certain extent. If the reader will try to sing it to the tune in the Appendix, he will find that in the first half he is led into several false accents; while the second half is quite unmanageable without altering the notes. There is, however, a form of the tune in Hawkins which is much farther off "the truth of the words," for it has exactly the right quantity of *notes*, but the *accents* are all as wrong as possible, thus:

> *Āll* pĕo-*plē* that *ŏn* earth *dō*
>
> *Dwĕll* sing tŏ *thĕ* Lŏrd with *chēerfŭl* vŏice.

It may be that this form of "Green Sleeves" was known better than the older one in Shakespeare's day.

"Carman's Whistle" (Appendix).

2 *Henry IV*, III, ii, 320. Falstaff soliloquizes on Shallow's lies concerning his wild youth.

> *Fal.* He [Shallow] came ever in the rearward of the fashion, and *sung those tunes* . . . that he heard the *carmen whistle*, and sware—they were his *fancies*, or his *goodnights*. . . . The *case of a treble hautboy* was a mansion for him, a court.

The "Carman's Whistle" was a popular Elizabethan tune, and was arranged as a virginal lesson by Byrd. This arrangement can be had most readily in Litolff's publication, *Les Maîtres du Clavecin*, and other similar collections, e.g. Augener's.

The "fancies" referred to above are the "Fantasies" already remarked on (chest of viols); and the "Goodnights" are songs *in memoriam*, or dirges.

"Callino Casturame." See *Henry V*, IV, iv, 4. The name is a corruption of the Irish "Colleen oge asthore." The tune and words are given in the author's *Shakespeare Music* (Curwen), p. 42, see also J. M. Gibbon's book, pp. 49–50.

"Fortune my foe" (Appendix). *Merry Wives of Windsor*, III, iii, 62:

Falstaff [*to Mrs. Ford*]. I see what thou wert, if Fortune thy foe were not; Nature thy friend.

This old tune is at latest of Elizabeth's time, and was sung to the ancient ballad of "Titus Andronicus." The first verse of "Fortune my foe" is as follows:

> Fortune my foe, why dost thou frown on me?
> And will thy favour never better be?
> Wilt thou, I say, for ever breed my pain,
> And wilt thou not restore my joyes again?

The "Sick Tune," referred to by Hero in *Much Ado about Nothing*, III, iv (just after Beatrice enters). Given in J. M. Gibbon's book, p. 106.

Ophelia's songs. *Hamlet*, IV, v (Appendix): "How should I your true love know?"; "Good morrow, 'tis St. Valentine's day"; "They bore him barefaste"; "Bonny Sweet Robin"; "And will he not come again?"

The one line of "Bonny Sweet Robin" is all that remains of the song, except the title, which is also the first line—viz. "My Robin is to the green-wood gone." The line Shakespeare gives would be the last. One tune to it is at any rate older than 1597. The Grave-digger's song in *Hamlet*, V, i, "In youth when I did love," is a version of part of a long set of

fourteen verses by Thomas Lord Vaux. Verse one
goes:

> I lothe that I did love,
> In youth that I thought sweete,
> As time requires for my behove
> Methinkes they are not mete.

Furness gives a bad traditional tune, very corrupt.
See also J. M. Gibbon, p. 36. Of course, any dismal-
sounding S.M. hymn tune would do for it.

Lastly, there are the old catches, "Hold thy peace,"
sung by Toby, Sir Andrew, and Feste in *Twelfth
Night*, II, iii; "Jack boy, ho boy, news, The cat is in
the well," etc., referred to by Grumio in *Taming of
the Shrew*, IV, i, 42; besides "Flout 'em and scout
'em," sung by Stephano, Trinculo, and Caliban in
Tempest, III, ii; and "What shall he have that
kill'd the deer?" for the foresters in *As You Like It*,
IV, ii, 5. The original music of the first two, probably
much earlier than Shakespeare, is in the Appendix.
A round for four voices by John Hilton (Mus.B. of
Cambridge, 1626, and organist of St. Margaret's,
Westminster, in 1628), to "What shall he have," is
probably the first setting, and may be seen in Rimbault, p. 19. Purcell (1675) set "Flout 'em" as a
catch for three voices, which is in Caulfield's *Collection
of Shakespeare Vocal Music*, 1864. These last two
are poor specimens of catches, so they are not printed
here. (The proper reading of "Flout 'em," in the

Quartos and First Folio, is "Flout em and *cout* 'em! and *skowt* 'em, and flout 'em! Thought is free.")

The following passage contains a large quantity of the history of songs in the sixteenth century, and is one of the most important to be found in Shakespeare. Autolycus sells ballads "of all sizes" among his wares; the country folk, Mopsa, Dorcas, and the Clown, buy them, and afterwards sing them; and the rustic servant distinctly prefers the pedlar's vocalization to their accustomed "tabor and pipe," or even to the "bagpipe."

Winter's Tale, IV, iii, 181:

Servant. O master! if you did but hear the *pedlar* at the door, you would *never dance again after a tabor and pipe*; no, the *bagpipe* could not move you. He *sings several tunes* faster than you 'll tell money; he utters them as he had *eaten ballads*, and all men's ears grew to his tunes.

Clown. He could never come better: he shall come in. *I love a ballad* but even too well; if it be doleful matter, merrily set down, or a very pleasant thing indeed, and sung lamentably.

Serv. He hath *songs*, for man or woman, *of all sizes.* . . . He has the prettiest *love-songs* for maids; so without bawdry, which is strange; with such *delicate burdens* of "dildos" and "fadings," "jump her and thump her"; . . . "Whoop, *do me no harm, good man.*"

Line 212:

Clown. Pr'ythee, bring him in, and let him *approach singing.*

Perdita. Forewarn him, that he use *no scurrilous words* in 's tunes.

Line 259:

Clown [*to Autolycus*]. What hast here? *ballads?*

Mopsa. 'Pray now, buy some: I love a *ballad in print*, o' life, for *then we are sure they are true*.

Autolycus. Here's one to a *very doleful tune* . . . [of a usurer's wife].

Line 273:

Clown. Come on, lay it by: and let 's first see *more ballads*. . . .

Aut. Here's *another ballad, of a fish*, that . . . sung this ballad against the hard hearts of maids: . . . the ballad is *very pitiful*, and as true.

Line 285:

Clown. Lay it by too: another.

Aut. This is a *merry ballad*, but a *very pretty* one.

Mop. Let 's have some merry ones.

Aut. Why, this is a passing merry one, and *goes to the tune of* "Two maids wooing a man": there's scarce a maid westward but she sings it: *'tis in request*, I can tell you.

Mop. We can *both* sing it: if *thou 'lt bear a part* [i.e. Autolycus], thou shalt hear; 'tis in *three parts*.

Dorcas. We had the *tune* on 't a month ago.

Aut. *I can bear my part*; you must know, *'tis my occupation*: have at it with you.

[They sing "Get you hence," in three parts.]

Clown. We 'll have the song out anon *by ourselves*.

Line 328:

Servant. Master, there is *three* carters, *three* shepherds, *three* neat herds, *three* swine herds, that have made themselves all *men of hair*: they call themselves *Saltiers*; and they have a *dance*, which the wenches say is a gallimaufry of gambols, because they are not in 't. . . .

·   ·   ·   ·   ·

Line 609:

Aut. My clown (who wants but something to be a reasonable man) grew so in love with the wenches' *song*, that he would not stir his pettitoes, *till he had both tune and words*.

The tabor and pipe, in the servant's first speech, were common popular instruments.[1] The tabor, of course, was a small drum, which was used as accompaniment to the pipe, a large whistle with three holes, but with a compass of eighteen notes. In its curiously disproportionate compass, it may be compared to the modern "picco" pipe of the music shops. Mersennus (early seventeenth century) mentions an Englishman, John Price, who was an accomplished player. Mersennus says the tabor pipe was in G. This probably means it was about eighteen inches long, and its lowest available note "g" above the treble staff. This agrees with the picture from a contemporary woodcut (in Calmour's *Fact and Fiction about Shakespeare*) showing William Kemp, one of Shakespeare's fellow-actors, dancing a morris to the tabor and pipe. The pipe is as long as from mouth to waist, i.e. about eighteen inches. A similar woodcut in *Orchésographie* (1588) makes the pipe perhaps one foot nine inches, and the head of the drum nine or ten inches across. The French tabor has a "snare."

[1] See *Don Quixote*, Part II, chap. xx, where a dance is accompanied by "cuatro diestros tañedores de tamboril y flauta"—four skilful players on tabor and flute.

The tabor-pipe is called *galoubet* in French, *Schwegel*
in German. A contemporary song speaks of Kemp:

> Since Robin Hood, Maid Marian,
> And Little John are gone a;
> The Hobby Horse was quite forgot
> When Kempe did dance alone a.
> He did labour after the Tabor
> For to dance, then in to France
> He took pains to skip it, etc.

For the "hobby horse" line, see *Hamlet*, III, ii, 136,
where Hamlet speaks to Ophelia about short memories
of the dead, "whose epitaph is":

> For O, for O, the hobby horse is forgot.

The tabor and pipe is played on by Ariel; see a
subsequent quotation from the *Tempest*, III, ii, 126
and 152. Also *Much Ado about Nothing*, II, iii, 13;
and the tabor alone, in *Twelfth Night*, III, i.

The bagpipe [1] was very similar to the instruments
of that name which still exist. At the present
moment there are four kinds in use: Highland Scotch,
Lowland Scotch, Northumbrian, and Irish. The last
has bellows instead of a "bag," but in other ways
they are very much alike. They all have "drones,"
which sound a particular note or notes continually,
while the tune is played on the "chanter." Shake-

---

[1] The bagpipe appears on a coin of Nero. Also there is a figure of
an *angel* playing it, in a crosier given by William of Wykeham to
New College, Oxford, in 1403.

speare himself tells us of another variety—viz., the
Lincolnshire bagpipe, in 1 *Henry IV*, I, ii, 76, where
Falstaff compares his low spirits to the melancholy
"drone of a Lincolnshire bagpipe." [1]

The servant's second speech refers to the character
of the words of the popular ballads, which were too
often coarse and even indecent.

"Love-songs" are quite a large class, frequently
referred to. For instance, *Two Gentlemen of Verona*,
II, i, 15:

> *Valentine*. Why, how know you that I am in love?
>
> *Speed*. Marry by these special marks: first, you have
> learn'd . . . *to relish a love song*, like a robin-redbreast . .

Romeo and Juliet, II, iv, 15.

> *Mercutio*. Alas, poor Romeo! he is already dead; . . . shot
> through the ear *with a love-song*."

besides the passage from *Twelfth Night*, II, iii, quoted
farther on, where Feste offers Sir Toby and Sir
Andrew their choice between "a love-song, or a song
of good life."

The "delicate burdens," "dildos and fadings,"
"jump her and thump her," are to be found in
examples of the period. A round of Matthew White's,

[1] What is a "woollen bagpipe" (*Merchant of Venice*, IV, i, 55)?
Galpin connects "woollen" with Irish "uilleann" (elbow), meaning
the Irish pipes (from the action of the elbow in working the bellows).
My own poor guess is that "woollen" is just a misprint for "wooden."
Capell conjectures "wawling."

"The courtier scorns the country clowns" (date about 1600), has for its third and last line, "With a fading, fading, fading, fading," etc.[1] "Whoop, do me no harm" has already been spoken of.

In line 214 of the *Winter's Tale* passage, Perdita again takes precaution against Autolycus using "scurrilous words."

From line 285 to line 327 the passage refers to a very interesting department of sixteenth-century singing—viz., the habit of performing songs in three vocal parts. The singers were called Three-man songmen, and the songs themselves "Three-man songs," or "Freemen's songs." (*Freemen* is simply a corruption of *three - men*. Mr. Aldis Wright tells me it is analogous to *thills* or *fills*, for the shafts of a wagon. Rimbault, in the preface to *Rounds, Canons, and Catches*, is highly indignant with Ritson's "inconceivably strange notion" that Freemen is only a form of Three-men. Rimbault's reason was that *Deuteromelia* (1609) does contain Freemen's Songs in *four* parts. Mr. Aldis Wright also gives me the expression "*six*-men's song," from Percy's *Reliques*, also these definitions, which will all go to settle the matter:

Florio, *Italian Dictionary* (1611): "*Strambotti*,

---

[1] Dr. Grattan Flood has identified "fadings" with tunes for the *Rincce Fada*, an Irish country dance. Cf. Ben Jonson's *Irish Masque* (1613): "And show tee how tey can foot te fading and te fadow, and te phip a' Dunboyne, I trow."

country gigges, rounds, catches, virelaies or *threemen's songs*." "*Cantarini*, such as sing *threemen's songs*." "*Berlingozzo* . . . Also a drunken or *threemen's song*."

Cotgrave, *French Dictionary* (1611): "*Virelay*. m. A virelay, round, *free*mans song."

Giraldus Cambrensis (1188) says that singing in parts was indigenous to the parts beyond the Humber, and on the borders of Yorkshire. Three-man singing may still be heard (not as an exotic) in Wales and the West of England. This last is referred to in the above passage, "There's scarce a maid westward but she sings it" — viz. the song in three parts.

Shakespeare is strictly historical in making a pedlar, and two country lasses, capable of "bearing a part" in a composition of this sort.

A terrible story about "men of hair" is told— of what happened on 29 January, 1392–3, at the Hôtel de Saint-Pol, Paris. King Charles VI and eleven courtiers were dressed in tight-fitting garments of linen covered with fine flax, to look like hairy savages, and were dancing before the queen, the Duchess of Berri, etc., when the Duke of Orleans, trying to see who the maskers were, held a torch too near, and five of them (chained together) got on fire, the flax catching flame easily . . . two died on the spot, and two more a few days after, in great agony. One, Jean de Nantouillet, broke the chain, and ran to the buttery, where he flung himself into a tub of water for dishwashing, and so saved his life.

Every illuminated copy of Froissart has a picture of this.

The three-man songmen are more particularly described in *Winter's Tale*, IV, ii, 41:

Clown. She hath made me four-and-twenty nosegays for the *shearers*; *three-man songmen all, and very good ones,* but they are *most of them means and bases;* but *one Puritan* amongst them, and he *sings psalms to hornpipes.*

These musical harvesters square closely with the account given in the Introduction, of music amongst the lower classes.   Here were twenty-four good glee singers, with the single defect that their tenors were very weak, "most of them means [altos] and bases." The Puritan was most accommodating, and his singing the words of psalms to the tune of the hornpipe would tend to show that the Old Adam was not all put away as yet. His compromise with his conscience reminds one of the old stories (all too true) of church singers in the fifteenth and sixteenth centuries, who would sing the by no means respectable words of popular comic ditties to the solemn strains of the mass "l'Homme armé," or whatever well-known melody the music happened to be constructed on.

An example of a three-man song will be found in the Appendix, "We be soldiers three."

Shakespeare also alludes to *sacred* part-music.

Falstaff, by his own account, was a notable singer of anthems, in which holy service he had lost his voice; he was familiar with members of the celebrated choir of St. George's Chapel at Windsor; and was not above practising the metrical psalmody in his sadder moments.

2 *Henry IV*, I, ii, 182:

Chief Justice. Is not your *voice broken*, your wind short, your chin double, your wit single, and every part about you blasted with antiquity, and will you yet call yourself young? Fie, fie, fie, Sir John!
Falstaff. My lord . . . For my *voice*, I have *lost it with* hollaing, and *singing of anthems.*

Ibid., II, i, 88:

Hostess. Thou didst swear to me . . . upon Wednesday in Wheeson week, when the prince broke thy head for liking his father to a *singing-man of Windsor.*

Ibid., II, iv, 137. Falstaff laments the degeneracy of the times:

Fal. There live not three good men unhanged in England, and one of them is fat, and grows old; God help the while! a bad world, I say. *I would I were a weaver; I could sing psalms or anything.*

This last sentence connects curiously with Sir John Oldcastle, the leader of the Lollards, who were noted for their psalm-singing. These Flemish Protestants, who had fled from the persecutions in their own country, were mostly *woollen* manufacturers, and

were distinguished for their love of psalmody, throughout the western counties, where they settled.   Hence
the   allusion   to   "weavers"   and   "psalms."   But
according to the Epilogue of 2 *Henry IV*, "Oldcastle died a martyr, and *this is not the man.*"

Falstaff knew well what a ballad was, too—as the
following shows.

Ibid., II, ii, 43:

Fal. [*to Hal*]. Go hang thyself in thine own heir-apparent
garters! If I be ta'en, I'll peach for this.   An I have not
ballads made on you all, and *sung to filthy tunes*, let a cup of
sack be my poison.

Two other worthy knights claim our attention in
the next quotation, which contains many interesting
allusions. *Inter alia*, Sir Toby gives Feste sixpence
to sing a song; Sir Andrew follows it up with a
"testril."   The Clown then sings them "O mistress
mine." (For the original music see Sir J. F. Bridge's
Shakespeare Songs, Novello, a collection which every
reader of Shakespeare ought to have.) Then, at
Sir Toby's suggestion, they all three sing a catch,
or, in his own words, "draw *three* souls out of *one*
weaver," an allusion to the *three* vocal parts which
are evolved from the *one* melody of the catch, as
well as a sly reference to "weavers" singing catches.
(See Introduction.) They sing "Thou Knave," for
which see the Appendix. It is not a good catch,
but sounds humorous if done smartly, and perhaps

its very roughness suits the circumstances. Next, after Maria's entrance, Toby either quotes the titles, or sings odd lines of four old songs (see Appendix); and when Malvolio comes in, furious with the noise they are making in the middle of the night, he applies precisely those epithets to their proceedings that our histories lead us to expect—e.g. "gabbling like *tinkers*," "*alehouse*," squeaking out your "*coziers'* catches" ("cozier" is "cobbler"). Sir Toby's puns on "keep time" in lines 94 and 115 ought not to be missed. To "keep time" is almost the only virtue a catch singer *must* have.

Twelfth Night, II, iii, 18:

Sir Toby. Welcome, ass. Now *let's have a catch.*
Sir Andrew. By my troth, the fool has an *excellent breast.* I had rather than forty shillings I had such a leg, and so *sweet a breath to sing,* as the fool has.

Line 30:

Sir Andrew. Now, *a song.*
Sir Toby. Come on; there is *sixpence* for you; let's have *a song.*
Sir Andrew. There's a *testril* of me too; if one knight give a——
Clown. Would you have a *love-song,* or a *song of good life*?
Sir Toby. A love-song, a love-song.
Sir Andrew. Ay, ay; I care not for good life.
                    [Clown sings "O mistress mine."]
Sir Andrew. A mellifluous voice, as I am true knight.
Sir Toby. A contagious breath.
Sir Andrew. Very sweet and contagious, i' faith.

Sir Toby. *To hear by the nose*, it is *dulcet in contagion.*
But shall we make the welkin dance indeed? Shall we rouse
the night-owl in a *catch*, that will *draw three souls out of
one weaver*? Shall we do that?

Sir Andrew. An you love me, let's do't: I am *dog at a
catch.*

Clown. By 'r lady, sir, and *some dogs* will catch well.

Sir Andrew. Most certain. Let our *catch* be, "Thou
Knave."

Clown. "Hold thy peace, thou knave," knight? I shall
be constrained to *call thee knave*, knight.

Sir Andrew. 'Tis not the first time I have constrained one
to call me knave. *Begin*, fool: it begins, "*Hold thy peace.*"

Clown. I shall never begin, if I hold my peace.

Sir Andrew. Good, i' faith. Come, begin.

[*They sing a catch.*[1]

Enter Maria.

Maria. What a caterwauling do you keep here!

.   .   .   .   .

Sir Toby. My lady's a Cataian; we are politicians; Mal-
volio's a Peg-a-Ramsey, and "*Three merry men be we.*"
. . . Tilly-valley, lady! [Sings.] "There dwelt a man in
Babylon, lady, lady!"

.   .   .   .

Sir Toby. [*Sings.*] "O! the twelfth day of December"——
Maria. For the love o' God, peace!

Enter Malvolio.

Mal. My masters, are you mad? or what are you? Have
you no wit, manners, nor honesty, but to *gabble like tinkers*
at this time of night? Do ye make an *alehouse* of my lady's
house, that ye squeak out your *coziers' catches* without any

[1] It is worth notice that "Hold thy peace" can be sung by two
voices only.   This would be convenient to Sir Toby and Clown, for
Sir Andrew was probably quite incompetent.

mitigation or remorse of voice? Is there no respect of place, persons, or *time* in you?

Sir Toby. We did keep time, sir, in our catches. Sneck up!

Lines 103–14, another song, "Farewell, dear heart" (see p. 70, and Appendix).

It is perhaps necessary to explain the nature of a catch, or round, more clearly. The two names were interchangeable in the sixteenth and seventeenth centuries. It was not till quite modern times that "catch" implied a necessary quibble in the words, deliberately arranged by the writer. First, a catch or round of the best type of Elizabethan times consisted of *one melody*, generally perfectly continuous. Secondly, the said melody was always divisible into a certain number of *equal sections*, varying from three to six, or even eight; and as many sections as there were, so many voices were necessary. Thirdly, each of these equal sections was deliberately arranged so as to make *harmony* with every other.

Here are the words of a round of the seventeenth century, which is divisible into three equal sections, and therefore is sung by three voices:

1. Cuckoo! Hark! how he sings to us.
2. Good news the cuckoo brings to us;
3. Spring is here, says the cuckoo.

Now, the way for three persons, A, B, and C, to sing this catch or round is as follows:

A begins (see above, line 69, "*Begin*, fool") line 1,

and immediately proceeds to line 2; at this very
instant, B in his turn begins line 1, and acts similarly.
When A has reached the first syllable in line 3, and
B is at "Good" in line 2, it is time for C also to
begin at line 1.   As soon as A has finished line 3, he
begins again; and so on with the others—"round"
and "round" till they are tired of "catching" each
other up.

Thus when they are all three fairly set going, their
one melody produces *three-part* harmony, and the
catchers have drawn "three souls out of one
weaver."[1]

The principle in all other catches or rounds is
exactly the same, however great the number of parts.

In the following we have another case of catch-
singing.   The original music of "Flout 'em" has not
come down to us.

Tempest, III, ii, 122:

Stephano. Come on, Trinculo, *let us sing.*
          [They sing a *catch*, "Flout 'em and scout 'em."]
Caliban. That's not the tune.   [Very likely, as they were
tipsy.]
                    [*Ariel plays the tune on a tabor and pipe.*
Ste. What is this same?
Trin. This is the *tune of our catch*, played by the picture
of Nobody.

·   ·   ·   ·   ·

[1] Also, the more modern notion of humour in catches makes its
appearance here, for "Cuckoo" is heard, repeated incessantly.

Line 136:

Cal. Be not afeard; the isle is *full of noises,*
    Sounds, and *sweet airs,* that give delight, and hurt not.
    Sometimes a thousand *twangling instruments*
    Will hum about mine ears; and sometime *voices,* etc.
    Ste. This will prove a brave kingdom to me, where I *shall
have my music for nothing.*

Line 152:

I would I could *see* this taborer [Ariel]: he *lays it on.*

Also ibid., III, ii, 119:

Stephano, like most of the scamps in Shakespeare,
is a good musician.   He leads the catch, appreciates
Ariel's tabor playing (line 152), and is overjoyed to
think that he will have all his music "for nothing"
(line 145) in the magical isle.

Finally, in the *Taming of the Shrew,* we have the
title of another old catch, of which the music has
survived—viz., "Jack, boy."

Taming of the Shrew, IV, i, 42:

Curtis. Therefore, good Grumio, the *news.*
    Grumio. Why, "*Jack, boy! ho, boy!*" and as much *news*
as thou wilt.

The words of this catch, which takes four voices,
are:

> Jack, boy, ho! boy, news;
> The cat is in the well,
> Let us ring now for her knell,
> Ding, dong, ding, dong, bell.

The music (see Appendix), like that of so many other catches, is anonymous, and is of some date long before Shakespeare.

As You Like It, V, iii, 7:

Touchstone. By my troth, well met. Come, sit, sit, and a *song*.

2 *Page*. We are for you; sit i' the middle.

1 *Page*. Shall we *clap into 't roundly, without hawking, or spitting*, or *saying we are hoarse*, which are the *only prologues to a bad voice*?

2 *Page*. I' faith, i' faith; and *both in a tune*, like two gipsies on a horse.

(Song follows, "It was a lover."   Could be sung as a *two*-part madrigal quite easily.   See my *Shakespeare Music* [Curwen], where the song is arranged for two voices, as Shakespeare says, "two gipsies on a horse." See also Bridge's *Shakespeare Songs*, for Morley's original setting.)

Touch. Truly, young gentlemen, though there was no great matter in the ditty, yet the *note* was very *untuneable*.

1 *Page*. You are deceived, sir; *we kept time*; we *lost not our time*.

Touch. By my troth, *yes*; I count it but *time lost* to hear such a foolish song. God be wi' you; and *God mend your voices*. Come, Audrey.

The First Page's speech at line 9 is most humorously appropriate. "Both in a tune, like two gipsies on a horse," is a quaint description of a duet. There is yet another pun on "lost time" in lines 36–8.

Jaques's cynicism comes out even in his limited dealings with music.

Ibid., IV, ii, 5:

Jaques. Have you no *song*, forester, for this purpose?
2 *Lord.* Yes, sir.
Jaq. Sing it; *'tis no matter how it be in tune, so it make noise enough.*

Song follows, "What shall he have, that kill'd the deer?" Rimbault, p. 19. Music by Hilton, who took his Mus.B. in 1626, and published *Ayres or Fa Las* in 1627. This round for the four foresters can scarcely be the setting known to Shakespeare.

This section will conclude with two quotations about singing of a more serious turn.

Twelfth Night, II, iv, 1:

Duke. Give me some music.—Now, good morrow, friends.
　Now, good Cesario, but that *piece of song*,
　That *old and antique song*, we heard last night;
　Methought, it did relieve my passion much,
　More than *light airs* . . .
　Come; but *one verse.*
Curio. He is not here, so please your lordship, that should sing it.
　Duke. Who was it?
　Cur. Feste, the jester, my lord . . .
Duke. Seek him out, and *play the tune the while.*
　[*To Cesario.*]—How dost thou like *this tune?*

Line 20:

Viola. It *gives a very echo* to the seat
　Where love is thron'd.

Line 43:

Duke. Mark it, Cesario; *it is old, and plain* . . .
                          [Clown sings "Come away, death."]

Line 67:

Duke. There's for thy pains.
Clown. No pains, sir ; I take pleasure in singing, sir.
Duke. I'll pay thy pleasure then.

"Light airs" in line 5 means "vain fiddling jigs"—
i.e. lively instrumental music.   Lines 20–2 and 43
are worth remembering for many reasons.

The next and last passage requires no remark,
except that "organ pipe of frailty" means simply the
voice of the dying king.

King John, V, vii, 10.   Death of King John.

Prince Henry. Doth he still rage?
Pembroke.   He is more patient
   Than when you left him: *even now he sung.*
Prince Henry. O vanity of sickness! . . .
   . . . 'Tis *strange that death should sing.*
   I am the *cygnet* to this pale faint *swan,*
   Who *chants a doleful hymn* to his own death,
   And, from the *organ-pipe of frailty*, sings
   His soul and body to their lasting rest.

IV

THE history of serenades is as ancient as that of songs. At the end (1494) of the fifteenth century, Sebastian Brandt, a lawyer, wrote in Dutch his *Stultifera Navis*, or *Ship of Fools* (*Narrenschiff*), a severe satire on things in general, and popular amusements in particular. The book was afterwards translated into Latin, and thence, by Alexander Barclay (1508), into English. Here are some of the verses that treat of serenades in the year 1494:

> The furies fearful, sprong of the floudes of hell,
> Bereft *these vagabonds* in their mindès, so
> That by no meane can they abide ne dwell
> Within their houses, but out they nede must go;
> More wildly wandring then either bucke or doe.
> Some with their *harpes*, another with their *lute*,
> Another with his *bagpipe*, or a foolishe *flute*.

> Then measure they their *songs* of melody
> *Before the doores of their lemman deare*;
> Howling with their foolishe songe and cry,
> So that their lemman may their great folly heare:
> But yet moreover these fooles are so unwise.

95

That *in cold winter* they use the same madness.
When all the houses are lade with snowe and yse,
O madmen amased, unstable, and witless!
What pleasure take you in this your foolishness?
What joy have ye to wander thus by night,
Save that *ill doers alway hate the light?*

Another verse explains that not only the foolish young men of *low* birth were given to this practice, but also:

States themselves therein abuse,

.   .   .   .   .

With *some yonge fooles of the spiritualtie*:
The foolish *pipe* without all gravitie
Doth eche degree call to his frantic game:
The darkness of night expelleth feare of shame.

Brandt had no great opinion of the music provided either.   He describes their singing before their lady's window:

One barketh, another bleateth like a shepe;
Some rore, some *counter*, some their *ballads fayne*:
Another from singing geveth himself to wepe;
When his soveraigne lady hath of him disdayne.

Finally—a Parthian shot:

Standing in corners like as it were a spye,
Whether that the wether be whot, colde, wet, or dry.

Thus, one hundred years before Shakespeare was born, serenades of voices and instruments were common, and in general practice by all classes of young men, and not only laymen, but also "yonge fooles of the spiritualtie."

The instruments mentioned are such as were still in use in Shakespeare's time—viz., harp, lute, "foolish" pipe, bagpipe, and "foolish" flute, besides the several varieties of song, which evidently included both solo and part singing—"feigned" ballads for a single voice (ballads, that is, in the more refined "keys" of "musica ficta"), and "countering," which implies that two voices at least took part.

The following passage is an example of this nocturnal serenading by a company of gentlemen.

Two Gentlemen of Verona, III, ii, 83:

Proteus. Visit by night your lady's chamber window
   With some *sweet concert*: to their *instruments*
   Tune a *deploring dump.* . . .
Thurio. And thy advice this night I'll put in practice.
   Therefore, sweet Proteus, my direction-giver,
   Let us into the city presently,
   To sort some gentlemen well skilled in music.

Proteus advises Thurio to get a "consort" (probably of viols) to play a "dump" under Silvia's window. He goes to arrange for some of his friends to attend for this purpose. The serenade takes place in the next Act, where, in the second scene, line 17, it is called "evening music," but does not include the "dump," for Thurio has "a sonnet that will serve the turn," so they sing "Who is Silvia?"

Here is the passage, which is full of quibbles on musical terms.

Ibid, IV, ii, 16:

Proteus. . . . Now must we to her window,
And give *some evening music to her ear.*

Line 24.

Thurio. . . . Now, gentlemen,
Let's tune.

Line 28:

Host [*to Julia, in boy's clothes*].   I 'll bring you where you shall *hear music,* and see the gentleman that you ask'd for.
Jul. But shall I *hear him speak?*
Host. Ay, that you shall.
Jul. That will be music.

Line 54:

Host. How do you, man [i.e. Julia]? the *music likes you not.*
Jul. You mistake: the *musician* [i.e. Proteus] likes me not.
Host. Why, my pretty youth?
Jul. He *plays false,* father.
Host. How? *out of tune on the strings?*
Jul. Not so; but yet *so false,* that he grieves my very *heart-strings.*
Host. You have a *quick ear.*
Jul. Ay; I would I were deaf! it makes me have a *slow heart.*
Host. I perceive, *you delight not in music.*
Jul. Not a whit, when it *jars* so.
Host. Hark! what fine *change* is in the music.
Jul. Ay, that *change* [Proteus's unfaithfulness] is the spite.

Host [*misunderstanding again*]. You would have them *always* play but *one thing*?
Jul. I would always have *one* [Proteus] play but one thing.

Line 85.

Silvia [*from window*]. I thank you for your music, gentlemen.

The next passage is of a serenade in the early morning. Cloten arranges for the musicians (who seem in this case to be professional players) to give two pieces, one instrumental, followed by a song.

Cymbeline, II, iii, 11:

Cloten. I would this *music would come*. I am advised to give her *music o' mornings*; they say, it will penetrate.

Enter Musicians.

Come on: *tune*. If you can penetrate her with your *fingering*, so; we'll try with *tongue* too. . . . *First*, a very excellent good-conceited thing; *after*, a wonderful sweet air, with admirable rich words to it,—*and then* let her consider.

[The musicians perform "Hark! hark! the lark."]

So, get you gone. If this penetrate, I will consider your *music the better*; if it do not, it is a vice in *her ears*, which *horse-hairs*, and *calves'-guts* . . . can never amend.

In line 14, "fingering" and "tongue" correspond to "playing" and "singing." The first is to be a "fancy" for viols, "a very excellent good-conceited thing"; the second is the "wonderful sweet air," "Hark! hark! the lark."

"Good-conceited" means having many "conceits." These "fancies" were always contrapuntal, and the various artificial contrivances, answering of points, imitations, and what not, are referred to under this title.   The mention of "horse-hairs and calves'-guts" makes it clear that the instruments in this "morning music" were viols.

Another "evening music" is provided by Pericles, Prince of Tyre.

Pericles, II, v, 24.   Pericles, a musician (his education had been "in *arts* and arms," see II, iii, 82).

Per. All fortune to the good Simonides!
Sim. To you as much, sir! *I am beholding to you*
    For your sweet music this last night: I do
    Protest, my ears were never better fed
    With such *delightful pleasing harmony*.
Per. It is your grace's pleasure to commend,
    Not my desert.
Sim.   Sir, *you are music's master*.
Per. The worst of all her scholars, my good lord.

The next quotation is also of "morning music," but with a different object—not a lady, but a soldier, and of a somewhat rough and ready kind, to judge by the Clown's critical remarks.

The passage seems to indicate the use of bagpipes; for "they speak i' the *nose*" (see *Merchant of Venice*, IV, i, 48), and are called *wind*-instruments, and are mentioned under the name "pipes" in the last two lines.   Moreover, there is the remark of the Clown, represented here by dots, which is terribly appropriate to that instrument.

Othello, III, i. Cassio brings musicians to salute Othello:

Cass. Masters, *play here*; I will content your pains:
Something that 's brief; and bid "Good morrow, general."
[*Music*.

Enter Clown.

Clown. Why, masters, *have your instruments been in Naples*, that they *speak i' the nose* thus?
1 *Mus.* How, sir, how?
Clown. Are these, I pray you, called *wind*-instruments?
1 *Mus.* Ay, marry, are they, sir.

.   .   .   .   .

Clown. . . . masters, here's money for you; and *the general so likes your music*, that *he desires you*, for love's sake, *to make no more noise with it*.
1 *Mus.* Well, sir, we will not.
Clown. If you have *any music that may not be heard*, to 't again; but, as they say, to *hear* music the general does not greatly care.
1 *Mus.* *We have none such*, sir.
Clown. Then *put up your pipes in your bag*, for I 'll away. Go; vanish into air, away!

Pandarus appears to be a capital musician. In the following we find him questioning a musical servant of Priam's palace about some instrumental music which is going on within, "at the request of Paris." The servant amuses himself by giving "cross" answers to Pandarus's crooked questions, and in the process gets out two or three musical jokes— e.g. "*partly* know," "music *in parts*," "*wholly*, sir."

Farther on, Paris also plays on the term "broken" music.

Troilus and Cressida, III, i, 19:

Pandarus. What music is this?
Servant. I do but *partly* know, sir; it is *music in parts.*
Pan. Know you the *musicians?*
Serv. *Wholly*, sir.
Pan. Who play they to?
Serv. To the hearers, sir.
Pan. At whose pleasure, friend?
Serv. At mine, sir, and *theirs that love music.*

·   ·   ·   ·   ·

Line 52:

Pan. Fair prince, here is *good broken music.*
Paris. *You* have *broke* it, cousin; and, by my life, you shall make it whole again: you shall *piece* it out with a *piece* of your performance. [*To Helen.*] Nell, he [Pandarus] is *full of harmony.*

·   ·   ·   ·   ·

Line 95:

Pan. . . . Come, *give me an instrument.* [And at Helen's request, Pandarus sings, "Love, love, nothing but love."]

The custom of having instrumental music in taverns has already been referred to in the Introductory, near the end, where we learn that the charge for playing before the guests was twenty shillings for two hours in Shakespeare's time; also that a man could hardly go into a public house of entertainment without being followed by two or three itinerant musicians, who would either sing or play for his pleasure, while he was at dinner. Accordingly, we find Sir John Falstaff enjoying such a performance at the "Boar's Head," Eastcheap.

2 *Henry IV*, II, iv, 10:

> 1 *Drawer*. Why then, cover, and set them down: and see if thou canst find out *Sneak's noise*; Mistress Tearsheet would fain have *some music* [after supper, in a cooler room].

Line 227:

> *Page*. The *music* is come, sir.
> *Falstaff*. Let them *play*.—*Play*, sirs.

Line 380:

> *Fal*. *Pay the musicians*, sirrah.

The term "Sneak's noise" is most interesting. "Noise" means a company of musicians, and Mr. Sneak was the gentleman who gave his name to the particular band of instrumentalists who favoured the "Boar's Head."

Milton uses the word, in this sense, in the poem *At a Solemn Music*, where the "saintly shout" of the seraphic choir, with " loud uplifted angel - trumpets," "immortal harps of golden wires," and the singing of psalms and hymns, are collectively called "that melodious *noise*." Also in his *Hymn on the Nativity*, verse ix, he has "str\u00e8nged *noise*"— i.e. band of stringed instruments. The Prayer-book Version (Great Bible) of the Psalms, which was made in 1540, has the word in Ps. lxxxi, 1, "Make a cheerful *noise* unto the God of Jacob," and this in the next verses is said to consist of various musical instruments—e.g. the tabret, harp, lute, and trumpet. Also in the Authorized Version of 1611, Ps. xxxiii, 3, "Play skilfully with a loud *noise*," which was the instrumental accompaniment to a "new song." The same word is used in several other places, with the meaning of "music"—e.g. Pss. lxvi, 1; xcv, 1, 2; xcviii, 4, 6; c, 1; where "to make a joyful noise" is represented in the original by the same verb, except in one of the two cases in Ps. xcviii, 4.

The word was still in use in 1680, when Dr. Plot was present at the annual bull-running held by the minstrels of Tutbury, one of the features of which festivity was a banquet, with "a Noise of musicians playing to them."

The reputed cure of the tarantula's bite by music has already been mentioned. The next three examples are of somewhat similar cases.

In the first, Henry IV in sickness asks for music; the second is an account of Cerimon's attempt to rouse the half-drowned Thaisa with at least partial assistance from music; while the third represents Prospero using a solemn air to remove the magic spell which he had cast on Alonso and his other enemies.

2 *Henry IV*, IV, iv, 133. King Henry on his sick-bed:

King Henry. Let there be no noise made, my gentle friends;
　Unless some *dull and favourable hand*
　Will *whisper music* to my wearied spirit.
Warwick. Call for the *music* in the other room.

Pericles, III, ii, 87.   Cerimon's house at Ephesus.
Thaisa, cast up by the sea, is brought to life by his
directions.

Cerimon. Well said, well said; the fire and the cloths.
　The *rough and woful music* that we have,
　Cause it to sound, beseech you.
　The vial once more;—how thou stirr'st, thou block!—
　The music there! I pray you, give her air.

Tempest, V, i, 51.   Prospero employs music to
disenchant Alonso, Antonio, etc.

Pro. . . . and, *when I have required*
　Some heavenly music (which even now I do),
　To work mine end upon their senses . . .

Line 58:

　A solemn air : and the *best comforter*
　To an unsettled fancy, cure thy brains.

Next we have two examples of "Music at Home."
In the case of the Duke in *Twelfth Night*, it is "con-
certed" music, and the players seem to be performing
such a quaint old piece as "The Lord of Salisbury
his Pavin," by Gibbons, in *Parthenia*, the last "strain"
of which has just such a "dying fall" as is mentioned
in line 4.   The "dying fall" may be seen on p. 11 of
my *Shakespeare Music* (Curwen).   The bass repeats

a short phrase eight times without a break, falling eight degrees in the process.   The treble falls similarly in long notes from the top of the stave to the bottom. (See the remarks on the passage from *Lucrece* in Section I on the *technical* meaning of "strain.")

   Twelfth Night, I, i:

Duke. If *music* be the *food of love*, play on;
   Give me excess of it, that, surfeiting,
   The appetite may sicken, and so die.—
   That strain again! it had a *dying fall*:
   O! it came o'er my ear like the *sweet sound*
   That breathes upon a bank of violets,
   Stealing and giving odour.—Enough! no more:
   'Tis not so sweet now, as it was before.

Brutus's musical establishment is on a smaller scale than the Duke's.   He keeps a "good boy," who can sing to his own accompaniment on the lute, and is such a willing servant as to perform when almost overcome by sleep.

   Julius Cæsar, IV, iii, 256.   Brutus and his servant Lucius:

Bru. Bear with me, good boy, I am much forgetful.
   Canst thou hold up thy heavy eyes awhile,
   And *touch* thy *instrument* a *strain* or two?
Luc. Ay, my lord, an 't please you.
Bru.   It does, my boy.
   I trouble thee too much, but thou art willing.
            .   .   .   .   .
                              [Boy sings to lute.]

Bru. This is a *sleepy tune*: [*Boy drops off.*]—O murderous
  slumber!
Lay'st thou thy leaden mace upon my boy,
That plays thee music?—Gentle knave, good night;
I will not do thee so much wrong to wake thee.
If thou dost nod, thou *break'st thy instrument*:
I'll take it from thee; and, good boy, good night. . . .
                                [Ghost of Cæsar appears.]

Line 290.

Bru. Boy!—Lucius!—Varro! Claudius! sirs, awake!—
  Claudius!
Luc. [*asleep*]. *The strings*, my lord, *are false.*
Bru. He thinks he still is *at his instrument.*

In *Henry VIII*, III, i, is a case of the same kind.

Queen Katherine. Take thy *lute*, wench: my soul grows sad
  with troubles:
Sing, and disperse them, if thou canst. Leave working.
                                [Song, "Orpheus."]

The next passage brings us to another class of
music—viz., dirges, funeral songs, or "good-nights."
(See 2 *Henry IV*, III, ii, 322.)   In *Cymbeline*, IV, ii,
184, Cadwal (Arviragus) sounds an "ingenious
instrument" to signify Imogen's death. Polydore
(Guiderius) says they had not used it since their
mother died. The song, or more properly, duet,
which they sing directly after, in memory of Imogen,
may be taken in this connection. Unfortunately
there seems to be no musical setting of "Fear no
more the heat o' the sun" any older than 1740.

In the second of the following quotations "dirges" are mentioned by name.

Romeo and Juliet, IV, iv, 21:

Capulet. . . . Good faith! 'tis day:
   The county [Count Paris] will be here *with music* straight.

Scene v, line 84:

Cap. All things, that we ordained festival,
   Turn from their office to black funeral:
   Our *instruments* to *melancholy bells*;
   Our wedding cheer to a sad burial feast;
   Our *solemn hymns* to *sullen dirges* change.

In close connection with these funeral songs is the passage in *Henry VIII*, IV, ii, 77, where Queen Katherine, sick, requests her gentleman-usher to get the musicians to play a favourite piece of this class:

> . . . Good Griffith,
   Cause the musicians play me *that sad note*
   I named my knell, whilst I sit meditating
   On that celestial harmony I go to.
>   [*She sleeps; then, waking from the vision—*]
>   . . . Bid the music leave,
   They are harsh and heavy to me.

It would be of great interest if it were possible to identify Queen Katherine's "knell."

There is an old song, given in Chappell's *Popular Music*, "O Death, rock me to sleep," which might be the very one, for both music and words are singularly appropriate.   The refrain is as follows:

Tole on thou passing bell,
Ringe out my dolefull *knell*,
Let thy sound my death tell,
For I must die,
There is no remedye.

The song is most plaintive, and has a very striking
feature in the shape of a real independent accompaniment, which keeps up a continual figure of three
descending notes, like the bells of a village church.
Hawkins gives the poem, with certain variations,
and two extra verses at the beginning, the first
commencing:

Defiled is my name full sore,
Through cruel spite and false report;

and he says the verses are thought to have been
written by Anne Boleyn. Hawkins also gives music
(in four parts) to the first two verses, by Robert
Johnson, a contemporary of Shakespeare's. The
music of the song in Chappell is much older than
that; indeed, it is very possibly of Henry VIII's
time. The song provides Pistol with one of his
quotations (2 *Henry IV*, II, iv): "Then death rock
me asleep, abridge my doleful days."

V

THE history of dances is the history of the transition from pure vocal music to pure instrumental music. In the dances of the sixteenth century, we have the germs of the modern "sonata" form; and in the association of certain of them we have the first attempt at a sequence of different "movements," which finally resulted in the sonata itself.

The Elizabethan dances, especially the pavan, show us this development just at the point where instrumental music was dividing itself from vocal.

All the ancient dances were originally sung. In Grove's *Dictionary* (1890), vol. ii, p. 676, there is given the music of a *pavan*, in four vocal parts, with the words sung (copied from Arbeau's *Orchésographie*, 1588). Morley (*Practical Music*, 1597) mentions *ballete*, as being "songs which being sung to a dittie may likewise be danced." Again, he speaks of "a kind of songs . . . called Justinianas . . . all written in the *Bergamasca* language." See *Midsummer Night's Dream*, V, ii, 30, where Bottom is not so very in-accurate after all in asking Duke Theseus to "*hear a*

Bergomask dance between two of our company."
The same author also gives "*passamesos* with a dittie"
(i.e. sung), and distinguishes between these aforesaid
and "those kinds which they make *without* ditties."
(Passamesos are passing-measures—or passamezzo—
pavans, see *Twelfth Night*, V, i, 200.)

Hence it appears that in Elizabeth's reign some
dances were sung, and others were simply played.

Morley goes on to instance two particular dances
which were commonly associated together—viz.
pavans and *galliards* (*Twelfth Night*, V, i, 200; I, iii,
127, etc.; *Henry V*, I, ii, 252), the first of which he
says is for "grave" dancing, having three "strains,"
each containing 8, 12, or 16 semibreves (two beats
in a bar), which are each repeated; and that this
pavan is usually followed by a *galliard*, "a kind of
music made out of the other" (see Bull's pavan and
galliard, "St. Thomas Wake," in *Parthenia*), in
triple time, "a lighter and more stirring dance than
the *pavan*, and consisting of the same number of
straines."

The next passage from Morley is very interesting
when compared with the stage direction in *Timon
of Athens*, I, ii, 131, where a *masque* of *Ladies* as
Amazons enter the banqueting hall at Timon's house,
with *lutes* in their hands, *dancing and playing*. This
stage direction corresponds closely with Morley's
account: "The Italians make their *galliards* (which

they tearm *saltarelly*) plain" (i.e. alone; not as an appendage to the pavan, as in England), "and frame ditties to them, which in their *mascaradoes* they sing and dance, and manie times without any instruments at all, but instead of instruments they have *curtisans disguised* in men's apparell, who sing *and daunce* to their own songes."

The "French *bransle*," he says, is like the alman (allemande of Bach, etc.)—i.e. it "containeth the time of eight, and most commonly in short notes." This is the brawl, see *Love's Labour's Lost*, III, i, 9, and was one of several ways in which the country dance was danced, whether in a ring, or "at length," like our "Sir Roger."

He says that the "*voltes* and *courantes*" also are "like unto this," but are "danced after sundrie fashions" (he means, with different steps, but occupying the same rhythmical time, so that the same tune would do), "the *volte* rising and leaping, the *courant* travising and running, in which measure also our countrey dance is made, though it be danced after *another form* than any of the former."

"All these be made in *straines*, either two or three." See *Twelfth Night*, I, i, 4, "That *strain* again," or *Julius Cæsar*, IV, iii, 258, "Touch thy instrument a *strain* or two."

Christopher Sympson, the royalist soldier (1667), confirms Morley's statements as to the constitution

LUTES   *(See page* 54*)*

(From Canon Galpin's "Old English Instruments of Music")

No. 4 is a theorbo, 1619; No. 5 an arch-lute, seventeenth century. No. 3
is dated 1593.

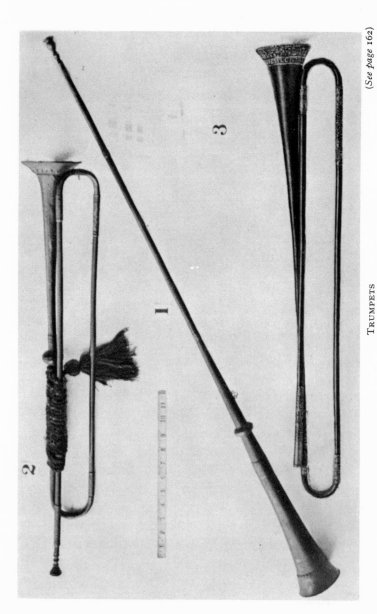

TRUMPETS

(From Canon Galpin's "Old English Instruments of Music")

(1) Buzine, 1460.   (2) Clarion, 1650.   (3) Field trumpet, 1651.

(See page 162)

and use of these dances. See his *Compendium*, p. 116, where he expressly states that pure instrumental music, "made only to delight the ear," is merely a development from dances.

He speaks of the association of pavan and galliard as being "in course." He spells the latter *giliard*, and says that it is, "according to its name" (see Skeat, *Etymological Dictionary*: "Spanish, *gallardo* (*ll=ly*), pleasant, gay, lively"), "of a loftly and frolick movement." Immediately afterwards, however, Sympson seems to forget his own remarks, for he says the name is derived from Gallia, "the country whence it came."

On page 117 he speaks of *corants, sarabands, jiggs, country dances*, etc., as "things so common in each one's ears" that he "need not enlarge his Discourse" to them.

There is a capital bit of patriotism on page 118, which deserves quoting, first, because at the time it was entirely justifiable; secondly, because it shows us that in 1667, instrumental music had at last decidedly parted company with vocal part-writing, and had an independent existence. "You need not seek Outlandish Authors, especially for Instrumental *Music*; no Nation (in my opinion) being equal to the *English* in that way; as well for their excellent as their various and numerous Consorts, of 3, 4, 5, and 6 Parts, made properly [on purpose] for Instruments, of all which (as I said) *Fancies* are the chief." For "Consort," see *Two Gentlemen of Verona*, III, ii, 83; and for "Fancies," 2 *Henry IV*, III, ii, 323.

Hawkins (1776) does not add much of interest to the above account of the Elizabethan dances, except (p. 704) that there is no authority for a jigg having generally a pointed (i.e. dotted) note at the beginning of every bar. There is, however, a "jegge" given in Stainer and Barrett's *Dictionary of Musical Terms*, dated 1678, where the "pointed" note is quite characteristic. This may be a more modern feature, for an undoubtedly ancient jig—viz. Dr. Bull's "King's Hunting Jigg"—not only has no dotted note, but is in common time, without even a tendency towards the rhythm of triplets. (Also see Appendix, "Cobbler's Jig," 1622; and "Kemp's Jig," in my *Shakespeare Music*, p. 28.)

Here is a most entertaining quotation from Selden,[1] dealing with fashionable court dances in Elizabeth's reign, and showing how things had gone from bad to worse in respect of dignity and state in dancing, under the Stuarts.

The court of England is much alter'd. At a solemn dancing, first you had the grave measures, then the Corantoes and the Galliards, and this kept up with ceremony; and at length to Trenchmore, and the Cushion-dance: Then all the company dances, lord and groom, lady and kitchen-maid,

[1] Selden's *Table Talk*, article "King of England," § 7.

no distinction. So in our court in queen Elizabeth's time,
gravity and state were kept up. In king James's time
things were pretty well. But in king Charles's time, there
has been nothing but Trenchmore and the Cushion-dance,
omnium gatherum, tolly polly, hoite cum toite.[1]

There are very many passages of interest, containing references to dances. The first one here given is
an instance (in Shakespeare's very text) of singing
a dance and dancing to it at the same time. Here
the *brawl* and *canary*, the first in alphabetical order,
are coupled together.

Love's Labour 's Lost, III, i, 9.

> *Moth*. Master, will you win your love with a *French brawl*?
> *Arm*. How meanest thou? *brawling in French*?
> *Moth*. No, my complete master; but to *jig off a tune* at
> the tongue's end, *canary to it* with your feet, . . . *sigh a note*
> and *sing a note*.

Two other examples of dancing to one's own singing
are *Midsummer Night's Dream*, V, ii, 25, and *Merry
Wives of Windsor*, V, v, 93.

The *brawl* was written in quick four-in-a-bar time.
There are several well-known tunes to it. (See Note
on Arbeau's *Orchésographie*, 1588.) The derivation
of the name is from the French, *bransle*, a totter,
swing, shake, etc., or perhaps from Old French

---

[1] Cf., for "Trenchmore," a passage in Burton (*Anatomy*, III, ii, 3):
"If once we be in love, young or old, though our teeth shake in our
heads, like virginal jacks . . . there is no remedy, we must dance
'Trenchmore' for a need, over tables, chairs, and stools, etc."

brandeler, to wag, shake, swing. Skeat thinks the original dance may have been a *sword* dance, and with this he connects the word brandish.[1]   It was danced, sometimes in a ring, holding hands, and sometimes "at length."

The *canary* (or canaries) was in $\frac{6}{8}$ time, and was a lively dance. (Stainer and Barrett's *Dictionary* gives one from *Orchésographie*, which is printed in my *Shakespeare Music*, p. 57, with its steps in $\frac{4}{4}$ time.) There are many examples by Lully and other Frenchmen of the seventeenth century. One of Lully's, in Lajarte's *Airs à Danser*, is dated 1666. There is no history of the name. Skeat says it is so called from the Canary Islands. Hawkins does not attempt to account for the title, but cunningly infers that it is of English origin because it has *not* got a foreign name. Also he mentions that Purcell wrote a canaries for his opera of *Dioclesian*, 1690. (See Note on *Orchésographie*.)

The canary is also alluded to in two other places, where the lively character of the dance is clear. Mr. Ford puns on "wine," "pipe," and "canary." Of course *he* means *whine*, *pipe* (for dancing to), and the *canary* that he meant Falstaff to dance.

Merry Wives of Windsor, III, ii, 83:

[1] This hardly seems a necessary theory. See the note on *Orchésographie*, where the "swinging" movement is fully accounted for.

Host. Farewell, my hearts. I will to my honest knight Falstaff, and drink *canary* with him.

Ford. [*Aside.*] I think, I shall drink in *pipe-wine* first with him; I 'll make him *dance.*

And next, Lafeu connects the canary with "spritely fire and motion."

All 's Well that Ends Well, II, i, 74:

Lafeu. . . . I have seen a medicine
That 's able to breathe life into a stone,
Quicken a rock, and make you *dance canary*
With spritely fire and motion.

There are two specially important passages which mention several dances at one time, so as to give some prominence to their special characteristics— viz. *Much Ado about Nothing*, II, i, 68, and *Twelfth Night*, I, iii, 118.

The budget of dances here named includes:

1. Cinque-pace, or Sinkapace. 2. Coranto, or Courante. 3. Galliard. 4. Jig (Scotch). 5. Measure.

Much Ado about Nothing, II, i, 68:

Beatrice. The fault will be in the *music*, cousin, if you be not woo'd *in good time*: if the prince be too important [importunate], tell him, there is *measure* in everything, and so *dance* out the answer. For hear me, Hero; wooing, wedding, and repenting, is as a *Scotch jig*, a *measure*, and a *cinque-pace*: the first suit is *hot and hasty*, like a *Scotch jig,* and full as fantastical; the wedding, *mannerly modest*, as a *measure*, full of *state and ancientry*; and then comes repentance, and with his bad legs falls into the *cinque-pace faster and faster* till he sink into his grave.

Twelfth Night, I, iii, 118:

Sir Toby. What is thy excellence in a *galliard*, knight?
Sir Andrew. 'Faith, I can *cut a caper*.

.   .   .   .   .

Line 123:

Sir Toby. Wherefore are these things hid? . . . why dost thou not *go to church in a galliard*, and *come home in a coranto*? My very *walk* should be a *jig*: . . . *sink-a-pace*. What dost thou mean? is it a world to hide virtues in? I did think, by the excellent constitution of thy leg, it was formed under the *star of a galliard*.

To take these five dances in order:

1. Cinquepace is the name of the original galliard. Praetorius (b. 1571) says a galliard has *five* steps, and is therefore called *cinque pas*. These five steps as described in the *Orchésographie*, 1588. See the Note on that work for the explanation of the steps of this and other Shakespeare dances.

Beatrice's description seems to connect the cinquepace with the tottering and uncertain steps of old age. "Repentance," she says, "with his *bad legs* falls into the cinquepace faster and faster, till he *sink* into his *grave*." [1]

2. Coranto is the Italian form of our country dance. The country dance is original in England,

[1] A pun on *greve*, one of the steps in the cinque pace. See p. 138. *Sink* is another pun, on *cinque*. Pictures showing the "greve droicte" and "greve gaulche" may be seen in my *Shakespeare Music* (Curwen), page xv. The steps of the cinquepace are explained on page 12 of the same book.

but under different foreign names has been called French or Italian. It means simply "country" or "rustic" dance. Skeat is entirely opposed to the derivation from "*contra* danza," with a supposed reference to two opposite lines of partners; and in this he is confirmed by Shakespeare, *Tempest*, IV, i, 138, "country footing." The old English name was "current traverse," and Morley (1597) speaks of the courant step as "travising and running," which would appear to connect the Italian word with *curro*. Sir John Davies (1570-1626), in his poem *Orchestra*, identifies rounds, corantos, measures, and some other dances with country dances. That is, whatever the rhythm or speed of the actual tune used, these variously named country dances could be performed to it. "Sir Roger de Coverley," our typical English country dance, is in *form* almost the same as the brawl, coranto, galliard, or measure. A courant by Frescobaldi (1591-1640) is in triple time. As for its "step," Davies says it is "on a triple dactile foot," "close by the ground with sliding passages." According to Sir Toby, it would be a quicker and gayer dance than the galliard, for he compares the walk to church to the latter; but the more lighthearted journey back to dinner he likens to the coranto. The jig would be even faster, for Sir Andrew's "very walk," that is, his *week-day* gait, was to be "a jig."

3. The galliard, in accordance with its derivation,

is properly described in *Henry V*, I, ii, 252, as a
"*nimble*" galliard.   This was extremely popular, both
as a virginal piece and for dancing.   There is quite a
long list of galliards by various composers, in the
Fitzwilliam Virginal Book.   There are several in
Parthenia (1611) by Byrde, Bull, and Gibbons.   They
are always in triple time, and consist of either two
or three strains of an even number of bars.

Sir Toby seems to connect a galliard with somewhat violent "capers."   He remarks on the "excellent
constitution" of Sir Andrew's leg, "it was formed
under the star of a galliard."   Sir Andrew com-
placently replies, "Ay, 'tis strong," upon which Sir
Toby proposes to the foolish knight to give an
example of his powers: "Let me see thee *caper*.
Ha! *higher*."   This capering or "sault majeur" was
also a feature of the "high lavolt" (lavolta) mentioned in *Troilus and Cressida*, IV, iv, 84, concerning
which Sir John Davies says:

> An anapæst is all their music's song,
> Whose first two feet are short, and third is long.

Also he calls the lavolta "a lofty jumping."   Morley
(1597) speaks of the volte, and says it is characterized
by "rising and leaping," and is of the same "measure"
as a coranto.   These statements do not all agree with
the *Orchésographie*.

4. Jigg (later gigue, and jig).   It is unlikely that

the name comes from giga (geige), a sort of fiddle in use during the twelfth and thirteenth centuries. The word is better related to "jack," the slip of wood holding the plectrum in the harpsichord or virginal, which jumps up and down, like the dancer. We may also remember the "jack" used by engineers, for instance, to lift a car from the ground. The oldest jigs are Scottish, and were "round dances" for a large number of people. As for the time of the jig tunes, those of the eighteenth century were certainly written in a triple rhythm, like $\frac{3}{8}$, $\frac{6}{4}$, or $\frac{12}{8}$. The jegge of 1678, mentioned above, is in quick $\frac{6}{4}$ time. But "The Cobbler's Jig" (Appendix), 1622, and a jigg by Matthew Locke, dated 1672, in his *Compositions for Broken and Whole Consorts of 2, 3, 4, 5, and 6 Parts*, are very decidedly in quick $\frac{4}{4}$ time, and have no such characteristics as a "dotted note" anywhere about them. Moreover, Bull's "The King's Hunting Jigg," is also in quick $\frac{4}{4}$ time, with a similar absence of dotted notes. This last example is probably earlier than 1600. At any rate it was a lively dance, as we can learn from Hamlet.

Hamlet, II, ii, 504. The First Player recites a speech.

Polonius. This is *too long*.
Hamlet. It shall to the barber's, with your beard.—Pr'ythee [to the *First Player*], say on: *he 's for a jig, . . . or he sleeps.*

5. Measure. Beatrice, in the quoted passage from

Much Ado about Nothing, gives a capital idea of the
relative speed of the Scotch jig and the measure.
The jig, she says, is like the lover's wooing, hot,
hasty, and fantastical; the measure, however, is like
the wedding, mannerly modest, full of state and
ancientry.

The term "measure" certainly seems to have been
used to signify a particularly staid and formal dance.
Selden (see above), at least, puts "grave measures"
at the sober beginning of his list, and so goes on, by
easy descent, through the more spirited coranto, and
tolerably lively galliard, to the lower depths of the
cushion-dance, which were reached towards the close
of the evening, when the grave and reverend elders
may be supposed to have gone to bed.

But, besides this, the word appears to have been
used generically, meaning merely "a dance." It was
certainly applied to the passamezzo, *and to other
country dances*. In *Henry VIII*, I, iv, 104, King
Henry says:

> . . . I have half a dozen healths
> To drink to these fair ladies, and a *measure*
> To lead 'em once again.

The next passage uses the word for a pun.
As You Like It, V, iv, 178:

Duke Senior. *Play music!* and you brides and bridegrooms all,
With *measure* heap'd in joy, to the *measures* fall.

Line 192:

Jaques. . . . So, to your pleasures;
  I am for other than for *dancing measures.*

A similar play upon the word is in *Richard II*,
III, iv, 6, where the queen asks her ladies to propose
some sport to drive away care.

1 *Lady.* Madam, we 'll dance.
Queen. My legs can keep no *measure* in delight,
  When my poor heart no *measure* keeps in grief:
  Therefore, no dancing, girl.

See especially the following, which holds a whole
string of quibbles:
  Love's Labour 's Lost, V, ii, 184.   Masked ball.

King of Navarre. Say to her, we have *measur'd* many miles,
  To tread a *measure* with her on this grass.
Boyet [*to the ladies*]. They say, that they have *measur'd*
    many a mile,
  To tread a *measure* with you on this grass.
Rosaline. It is not so.   Ask them how many inches
  Is in one mile: if they *measur'd* many,
  The *measure* then of one is easily told.
Boyet. If, to come hither, you have *measur'd* miles,
  And many miles, the princess bids you tell,
  How many inches do fill up one mile.
Biron. Tell her, we *measure* them by weary *steps*.

And line 209, *measure*.

Another dance that is frequently referred to is the
dump, the slow and mournful character of which
has already been explained in the notes on *Lucrece*,

1127.   As a serenade it is named in *Two Gentlemen of Verona*, III, ii, 83.   The nature of the steps of this dance is not certainly known.   Two features, however, may be guessed at—viz. a tapping of the foot at certain places, which may be inferred from the possible connection of the word with "thump"; and secondly, an alternation of a slow sliding step, interspersed with dead pauses, and a quicker movement, succeeded again by the slow step.   These last seem to be indicated by the music of "My Lady Carey's Dump." [1]   The character of the dump has given us the modern expression of "in the dumps," i.e. sulky; and this is also used commonly in Shakespeare.

In the next passage, Peter, Capulet's servant, speaks ironically of a "merry" dump, and quotes verse 1 of Richard Edwards's song, "When griping grief."   For an account of that song see Section III, about Songs and Singing.   In Peter's quotation, the dumps are "doleful."

The quibbles on "silver sound," "sweet sound," "sound for silver," "no *gold* for sounding," are further examples of Shakespeare's fondness for joking on musical matters.   Peter's reply to the Third Musician, "You are the singer; I will *say* for you," may be a

---

[1] A trustworthy copy of "My Lady Carey's Dump" is in my *Shakespeare Music* (Curwen), p. 7.   It is taken from the British Museum, Royal MS., appendix 58.   The date is 1510.

just reflection on Mr. James Soundpost's lack of
words, or perhaps indicates that the pronunciation of
singers even in that musical age was no better than it
is now.

The improvised names of the musicians are pointed
enough; Simon "Catling," referring to the material of
his viol strings; Hugh "Rebeck," the rebeck being
the ancient fiddle with three strings (the "smale"
ribible, which Absolon, the parish clerk in Chaucer,
used to play "songés" on, is supposed to be the same
instrument); and finally, James "Soundpost," which
wants no explaining.

The final remark of Musician 2 is delicious: "Tarry
for the mourners, and stay dinner."

Romeo and Juliet, IV, v, 96. After Juliet's
apparent death:

> *Exeunt Capulet, Lady C., Paris, etc.*

1 *Musician*. Faith, we may *put up our pipes*, and be gone.
Nurse. Honest good fellows, ah! *put up, put up*;
For well you know, this is a pitiful *case*.
1 *Mus*. Ay, by my troth, the *case* may be amended.

(See *Henry V*, III, ii, 42, about Bardolph and the
lute-case.)

> *Enter Peter.*

Peter. Musicians, O, musicians! "Heart's ease, Heart's
ease": O! an you will have me live, play "Heart's ease."
1 *Mus*. Why "Heart's ease"?
Peter. O, musicians, because my *heart itself* plays "My

heart is full of woe." O! play me some *merry dump*, to comfort me.

2 *Mus*. Not a *dump* we: 'tis no time to play now.

·   ·   ·   ·   ·   ·

Peter. Then will I lay the serving creature's dagger on your pate. I will carry no *crotchets*: I 'll *re* you, I 'll *fa* you. Do you *note* me?

1 *Mus*. An you *re* us, and *fa* us, you *note* us.

2 *Mus*. Pray you, put up your dagger, and put out your wit.

Peter. Then have at you with my wit. . . . Answer me like men:

> "*When griping grief the heart doth wound,*
> *And* DOLEFUL DUMPS *the mind oppress,*
> *Then music with her silver sound*" —

Why "silver sound"? why "music with her *silver* sound"? what say you, Simon *Catling*?

1 *Mus*. Marry, sir, because silver hath a *sweet sound*.

Peter. Pretty!—what say *you*, Hugh *Rebeck*?

2 *Mus*. I say, "silver sound," because musicians *sound for silver*.

Peter. Pretty too!—what say *you*, James *Soundpost*?

3 *Mus*. 'Faith, I know not what to *say*.

Peter. O! I cry you mercy; you are the *singer*: I will *say* for you. It is—"music with her silver sound," because musicians have no *gold* for sounding:

> "Then music with her *silver sound*
> With speedy help doth lend redress."   [*Exit*.

1 *Mus*. What a pestilent knave is this same!

2 *Mus*. Hang him, Jack! [Peter's names evidently all wrong.] Come, we 'll in here; tarry for the mourners, *and stay dinner*.   [*Exeunt*.

The hay, hey, or raye, seems to be mentioned

only once, viz., in *Love's Labour's Lost*, in the account of the preparations for the Pageant of the Worthies. Constable Dull proposes to accompany the dancing of the hay with a tabor, which may be taken as the common practice. Holofernes says Dull's idea is "most dull," like himself. The hay was a round country-dance, i.e. the performers stood in a circle to begin with, and then (in the words of an old direction quoted in Stainer and Barrett's *Dictionary*) "wind round *handing* in passing until you come to your places." See the Note on Arbeau's *Orchéso-graphie* for the steps and tune of the hay.

In Act V, scene i, of the Duke of Buckingham's burlesque play, *The Rehearsal* (1671), the earth, sun, and moon dance. As they dance, Bayes speaks: "Now the earth's before the moon; now the moon's before the sun; there's the eclipse again," which may be compared with Arbeau's description of the "Branle de la Haye," given on page 144 of this book.

Love's Labour's Lost, V, i, 148. Schoolmaster Holofernes & Co., arranging the Pageant of the Nine Worthies.

Dull. I'll make one in a *dance*, or so; or I will *play*
  On the tabor to the Worthies, and let them *dance the hay.*
Hol. Most dull, honest Dull.

The morrice-dance, or morris, was very popular in England and other countries in the sixteenth century.

Relics of it may still be seen in country places at certain times of the year. The very meagre celebrations of May Day, which might be seen in London not so long ago, are a survival of the ancient customs with which the morrice-dance was always associated. Hawkins gives this account of the morris: "There are few country places in this kingdom where it is not known; it is a dance of young men in their shirts, with bells at their feet, and ribbons of various colours tied round their arms, and slung across their shoulders. Some writers, Shakespeare in particular, mention a Hobby-horse and a Maid Marian, as necessary in this recreation. Sir William Temple speaks of a pamphlet in the library of the Earl of Leicester, which gave an account of a set of morrice-dancers in King James's reign, composed of ten men or twelve men, for the ambiguity of his expression renders it impossible to say which of the two numbers is meant, who went about the country; that they danced a Maid Marian, with a tabor and pipe, and that their ages one with another made up twelve hundred years."

[Temple's own words are quite clear, viz., that there were *ten* men who danced; a Maid Marian (makes eleven); and a man to play the tabor and pipe (makes twelve).]

The name Morrice means Moorish dance, or Morisco. Dances in extravagantly fantastical costumes, with such ornaments as feather head-dress, blackened faces, hairy garments, and so forth, were looked upon as "Moorish."

Two tunes, one a Moresca by Monteverde, 1608, and the other an English Morris, 1650, are given in the Appendix. Also see Note on *Orchésographie* for a Morisque.

The first of the two following passages connects the morris with May Day; the second with Whitsuntide, which is in May as often as not.

All's Well that Ends Well, II, ii, 20:

Countess. Will your answer serve fit to all questions?
Clown. As fit as . . . a pancake for Shrove Tuesday, a *morris* for *May-day*. . . .

Henry V, II, iv, 23:

Dauphin. And let us do it with no show of fear;
No, with no more, than if we heard that England
Were busied with a *Whitsun morris-dance*.

The pavan has been mentioned before, as the dance in duple time which preceded the galliard which was in a triple rhythm. It was a stately dance, with a stately name, for the derivation is most probably from *pavo*, a peacock, with a reference, no doubt, to the majestic strut and gay feathers of that bird. It was *de rigueur* for gentlemen to dance the pavan in cap and sword; for lawyers to wear their gowns, princes their mantles; and ladies to take part in the fullest of full dress, the long trains of their gowns being supposed to correspond in appearance and movement to the peacock's tail.

The only pavan mentioned by Shakespeare is the *passy-measures pavin*, otherwise known as passing-measures pavin, or passamezzo, or *pass 'e mezzo*, which last is the earliest form of the word.

Praetorius (b. 1571), however, says the *pass 'e mezzo* is so called because it has only *half as many steps* as a galliard. Thus the name is inverted, *mezzo passo*. Hawkins helps to confuse the matter by explaining that the galliard has *five bars or steps* in the first strain, and that the passamezzo has just half that number, and thus gets its name. No galliard ever had an uneven number of bars in any of its strains, so this account is difficult to reconcile.[1]

However, "pass' e mezzo," "step and a half," is the most trustworthy form of the name, and the Note on the *Orchésographie* of Arbeau (1588) makes all quite clear.

The passamezzo (or passy-measures pavin) tune in the Appendix has a similar construction to the ordinary pavan, the form of which has been explained

[1] I now believe that "passamezzo" was the name for a pavan played much too fast, so that the steps became much shortened. As to the galliard or *cinquepas* having *five* steps, that is correct, but the "sault majeure" must be remembered, making the number even once more. See my *Shakespeare Music* (Curwen), pp. xv, 12 and 56. This is in fact Arbeau's own explanation (1588) of "passemeze."

earlier in this section, i.e. it consists of regular "strains," which in their turn contain a certain *even* number of semibreves, or "bars." In the case given, the strains consist of *eight* bars each. This must be borne in mind, in connection with Sir Toby's drunken fancy about the surgeon, in the following passage.

Twelfth Night, V, i, 197:

> *Sir Toby* [*drunk, and with a bloody coxcomb*].   Sot, didst see Dick surgeon, sot?
> *Clown.* O! he's drunk, Sir Toby, an hour agone; his eyes were *set at eight* i' the morning.
> *Sir Toby.* Then he's a rogue, and a *passy-measures pavin*.

Toby, being only moderately sober, naturally feels indignant at the doctor's indiscretions in the same kind; and, quite as naturally, the Clown's remark about the latter's eyes brings this fantastic comparison into his head. The doctor's eyes were set *at eight*, and so is a pavan set "at eight." It is easy to see Sir Toby's musical gifts asserting themselves, confused recollections reeling across his brain, of that old rule in Morley about the right number of semibreves in a strain: "fewer then *eight* I have not seen in any *pavan* . . . Also in this you must cast your musicke by *foure*: . . . no matter how manie *foures* you put in your straine." Bull's pavan, "St. Thomas Wake," has two strains of *sixteen* bars each, i.e. two "eights." (Appendix.)

The last passage given here shows clearly that the

lavolta and coranto were considered exotic in England in Shakespeare's time.

The French ladies here recommend their runaway husbands and brothers to cross the Channel and try to earn a living by teaching French dances to the stately English. Probably the "English dancing-schools" in those days would think the solemn walk of the pavan quite as lively an amusement as good society could allow. There are other passages, too, which show that Shakespeare (or his characters) had a fine "insular" feeling against these "newfangled" fashions from France.

Henry V, III, v, 32.

Bourbon [*speaks of the mocking French ladies*].
They bid us to the *English dancing-schools*,
And teach *lavoltas high*, and *swift corantos*;
Saying, our grace is only in our heels,
And that we are most lofty runaways.

Note on Arbeau's "Orchésographie," 1588

This interesting book on the Art of Dancing was published at Mâcon in 1588. (The date on the title page is 1589.)[1] The author was Jehan Tabourot, but

[1] The title-page of the first edition gives no date; but the official permission to print the book, at the end, says 22 November, 1588. The place, Lengres. There was a second edition in 1596.

The Mâcon edition is 1589 (?). The reverend writer of the treatise has given an appropriate text from Eccles. iii, 4, on his title page, viz. "Tempus plangendi, et tempus *saltandi*."

A facsimile reprint was issued in Paris, 1888; a German edition by Czerwinski was published at Danzig, 1878; and an English edition was published by Cyril Beaumont in 1925.

his real name does not appear in the work, being anagrammatised into Thoinot Arbeau; and under the guise of Arbeau he is best known.

The treatise is written (like Morley's *Introduction to Practical Music*) in the form of Dialogue between Master (Arbeau) and Pupil (Capriol); and gives a most clear description of all the fashionable dances of the time, as far as words can do it; dance tunes in music type; and incidentally, many instructions as to the manners of good society.

As much light is thrown upon the dances which are mentioned in Shakespeare by this book, some of the principal descriptions will be given here, with the proper music.

On p. 25, Capriol (the Pupil) asks his Master (Arbeau) to describe the steps of the *basse-danse*. This was the "danse par bas, ou sans sauter," which was of the fifteenth century, was in triple time, and contained three parts: (*a*) *basse-danse*; (*b*) *retour de la basse-danse*; (*c*) *tordion*. This third part, or tordion, "n'est aultre chose qu'une gaillarde *par terre*"; i.e. the tordion of a *basse-danse* was simply a galliard *par terre*, without the leaping or "sault majeur."

Before Arbeau answers his pupil, he gives him some preliminary instruction as to the etiquette of the ball-room. He says: "In the first place . . . you should choose some virtuous damsel whose appearance pleases you (*telle que bon vous semblera*), take off your hat or cap in your left hand, and tender her your right hand to lead her out to dance. She, being modest and well brought up, will give you her left hand, and rise to follow you. Then conduct her to the end of the room, face each the other, and tell the band to play a *basse-danse*. For if you do not, they may inadvertently play some other kind of dance. And when they begin to play, you begin to dance."

Capriol. If the lady should refuse, I should feel dreadfully ashamed.

Arbeau. A properly educated young lady *never* refuses one who does her the honour to lead her out to the dance. If she does, she is accounted foolish (*sotte*), for if she doesn't want to dance, what is she sitting there for amongst the rest?

The Master then gives his pupil an account of the *basse-danse*, the first and second parts of which are composed of various arrangements of the following movements:

1. *La révérence*, marked with a big R.
2. *Le branle* (*not* the dance of that name), marked with b.
3. *Deux simples*, marked ss.
4. *Le double*, marked d.
5. *La reprise*, marked with a little r.

The *chanson*, i.e. the dance tune, was played on the flute, and accompanied by the *tabourin* or drum, which beats all the time. Every "bar" of the music is called either a *battement* of the drum, or a *mesure* of the *chanson*.

Now Arbeau explains the steps and time of each of the above movements.

1. R. This takes four bars. Begin with left foot forward, and in doing the *révérence*, half turn your body and face towards the Damoiselle, and cast on her "un gracieux regard."

2. b.[1] Also takes four bars. Keep the feet joined together, then for the 1st bar, swing the body gently to the left side; 2nd bar, swing to the right, while gazing modestly upon "les assistants"; 3rd bar, swing again to the left; and for the 4th bar, swing to the right side, looking on the Damoiselle with an "œillade desrobée, doulcement et discretement."

3. ss. 1st bar, left foot forward; 2nd bar, bring right foot up to the said left foot; 3rd bar, advance the right foot; 4th bar, join the left foot to the said right foot; "et ainsi sera parfaict le mouvement des deux simples."

N.B.—Always suit the length of your steps to the size of the room, and the convenience of the Damoiselle, who cannot with modesty take such big steps as you can.

4. d. 1st bar, advance left foot; 2nd, advance right

[1] The branle (not the dance, but as used here) is called *congedium* by Anthoine Arena. Arbeau thinks because the dancer appears about to take leave of his partner—i.e. *prendre congé*. See *Henry VIII*, IV, ii, 82, stage direction, "congee."

foot; 3rd, advance left foot; 4th, join right to left. For *two* doubles (dd) do it over again, but contrariwise, beginning with the right foot. For *three* doubles (ddd), the form of the third will be: 1st bar, advance left foot; 2nd, advance right foot; 3rd, advance left foot; 4th, "puis tumbera pieds joincts comme a esté faict au premier double." And thus (he carefully adds) the three doubles are achieved in twelve "battements et mesures du tabourin."

5. The reprise (r) is commonly found before the branle (b), and sometimes before the double (d) (see the *mémoires*). In it you have to cultivate a certain movement of the knees, or feet, or "les artoils seullement," as if your feet were shaking under you. 1st bar, "les artoils" of the right foot; 2nd bar, do.; 3rd bar, of the left foot; 4th, of the right foot again.

The *mémoire* of the movements of the *basse-danse*, i.e. its first part, is:

R b ss d r | d r b ss ddd r d r b | ss d r b C

The C means the *congé*, or "leave" which you must take of the Damoiselle, salute her, and keep hold of her hand, and lead her back to where you began, in order to dance the second part, namely the "retour de la basse - danse," the *mémoire* for which is:

b | d r b ss ddd r d r b | C

(The nine movements enclosed between the upright lines are the same in both parts.)

Capriol now remarks that he has been counting up,
and finds that the music of the *basse-danse* proper
(part 1) has twenty "fours" ("vingt quaternions"),
and the *retour* (part 2) has twelve "fours."

Arbeau then describes the tordion, which is part
3 of the *basse-danse*. He says it is still in triple
time, but "plus legiere et concitée," and does not
consist of "simples, doubles, reprises," etc., like the
first and second parts, but is danced almost exactly
as a galliard, except that it is *par terre*, i.e. without
any capers, and low on the ground, with a quick and
light step; whereas the galliard is danced *high*, with
a slower and weightier *mesure*.[1]

He gives the following tune, which will fit to *any*
of the innumerable diversities of galliard. If played
fast, it is a tordion, if slower, a galliard. (There are,
of course, no bars in the original.)

Tordion or Galliard (Cinquepace)

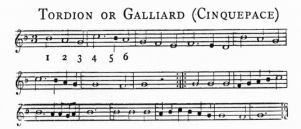

Here are the steps of the galliard, consisting of

[1] According to Rabelais (Book II, chap. v) one of the qualifications
of a Licentiate in Laws at Orleans University was "une basse danse
au talon."

five movements of the feet, and the caper, or "sault majeur." The five steps give the galliard the name of cinquepas.

1. Greve gaulche. ("Greve" is explained as a "coup de pied.")

2. Greve droicte.

3. „   gaulche.

4. „   droicte.

5. Sault majeur.

6. Posture gaulche.

1, 2, 3, 4, 6 are the "cinq" pas, and 5 is the characteristic leap or caper.

The next six minims are danced to the *revers*, which is just the same, except that the words "right" and "left" (*droicte* and *gaulche*) change places all the way down. Then repeat till the tune is finished.

Arbeau gives several other varieties of galliard, and another very good tune for it, called

"ANTHOINETTE." GALLIARD

The *sault majeur* in this tune would come in the middle of the semibreves in the first strain; at the

"dot" of the dotted minims in the 2nd and 3rd strains; or, again, in the middle of the semibreves in the same strains.

Of the pavan (commonly danced before the *basse-danse*), Arbeau says it is very easy, consisting only of "two simples and a double" advancing, and again "two simples and a double" retiring. It is (as we already know) in binary measure, and the careful Capriol (the pupil) once more joins in with his calculations of time, saying that he makes the pavan 8 measures (semibreves) "en marchant," and 8 measures "desmarchant."

The master now gives particular instructions about the form and manner of dancing the pavan. Noblemen dance these pavans and *basses-danses* "belles et graves," with cap and sword; others in long robes, "marchants honnestement, avec une gravité posée." And the damoiselles with an humble countenance, "les yeulx baissez, regardans quelquefois les assistans avec une pudeur virginale." Kings, princes, and "seigneurs graves," in dancing the pavan on great occasions, wear their "grands manteaux, et robes de parade." Also, queens, princesses, and ladies accompanying them, have their robes "abaissées et trainans," "quelquefois portées par demoiselles." The pavan on these occasions is called LE GRAND BAL, and the music is provided, not by simple flute and drum, but by "haulbois et saquebouttes," and they continue the tune until the dancers have made the circuit of the *salle* twice or thrice.

Besides this state dancing of pavans, this dance was used in *mascarade*, when triumphal chariots of gods and goddesses enter, or of emperors and kings "plains de maiesté."

On p. 29 ff., Arbeau gives the vocal pavan for four voices, "Belle qui tiens ma vie," which is quoted in Grove. The proper drum accompaniment, continued throughout the 32 bars ($\frac{2}{2}$), is— ♩ ♪ ♪ ♩ ♪ ♪ ♩ ♪ ♪ etc. He also gives seven more verses of words to it, and says if you do not wish to dance, you can play or sing it. Moreover, he adds, that the drum is not a necessity, but is good to keep the time equal; and that for dancing you may use violins, spinets, flutes, both traverse and "à neuf trous" (nine-holed flute, i.e. a recorder), hautboys, and, in fact, "all sorts of instruments"; or you may sing instead.

Arbeau's account of the passemeze, or passy-measures pavin of Shakespeare, is very simple. He says that the instrumentalists increase the speed of the pavan every time they play it through, and by the time it has reached the moderate speed of a *basse-danse*, it is no longer called pavan, but passemeze.

Besides the state pavan, and the passamezzo pavan, there is the "Pavane d'Espagne," which has some similarity to the canaries.

Arbeau says that some consider the name canaries

to be that of a dance in use in those islands. But he thinks it more likely to have originated in a ballet in a *mascarade*, where the dancers were clad as kings and queens "de Mauritanie," as savages, with various coloured feathers. He says it is danced by a gentleman and a lady, from opposite ends of the room, each advancing and then retiring in turn.

The steps and tune are as follows:

CANARIES

1. Tappement du pied gaulche, causant pied en l'air droit.
2. Marque talon droit (right heel).
3. Marque pied droit.
4. Tappement du pied droit, causant pied en l'air gaulche.
5. Marque talon gaulche (left heel).
6. Marque pied gaulche.

7–12 are the same again.

Then for the 2nd half, instead of the "tappements" at the minims, you should make "une greve fort haulte, rabaissée en tappement de pied trainé en derriere, comme si on marchoit dessus un crachat, ou qu'on voulust tuer une araignée." (Make a very high step, but instead of tapping the foot, scrape it back-wards, as if you were treading on spittle, or wanted to kill a spider.)

Arbeau gives seventeen different kinds of branle (brawl of Shakespeare) before coming to the "branle des Sabots," which is danced, two beats in a bar, four steps to the right, then four to the left, like the branle doubles; then two simples (see above), and three taps of the foot, and repeat.

BRANLE DES SABOTS, p. 88

<table>
<tr><td>Double gaulche.</td><td>
1. Pied gaulche largy (left foot forward).
2. „ droit approché (right foot up to the left).
3. Pied gaulche largy.
4. Pieds joincts (join feet).
</td></tr>
<tr><td></td><td>
5–8 are the same, "right" and "left" changing places, forming a "double droit."
</td></tr>
<tr><td>Simple gaulche.</td><td>
9. P. g. largy.
10. Pieds joincts.
</td></tr>
<tr><td>Simple droit.</td><td>
11. P. d. largy.
12. Pieds joincts.
</td></tr>
</table>

a. Tappement du pied droict.[1]
b.   Do.
c.   Do.

There is only one step to each semibreve, so the tune must have been played fast.

On p. 64 Arbeau treats of the lavolta ("high lavolt" of Shakespeare), which he says is a kind of galliard well known in Provence. One feature was that you had to keep turning round.

Capriol does not agree with these whirlings, for he immediately says: "Ces vertigues et tornoiements de cerveau me fascheroient."

AIR D'UNE VOLTE (LAVOLTA)

1. Petit pas, en saultant sur le gaulche, pour faire pied en l'air droict.
2. Plus grand pas du droict.
3. Sault majeur.

---

[1] In connection with this, it is perhaps of interest to compare *Don Quixote*, Part II, chap. xix, about the *zapateadores*, dancers who strike the soles of their shoes with the hand.

4. Posture en pieds joincts.

(Etc., all over again every two bars.)

The *sault majeur* of the "high lavolt" comes at the *semibreves* in this tune.

On p. 67 he gives the courante:

COURANTE

The movements are:

1, 2, simple gaulche; 3, 4, simple droit; and 5–8, a "double à gaulche." These terms have already been explained.

One of the many branles is the "Branle de la Haye," the hay of Shakespeare. Arbeau says: First the dancers dance alone, each separately; then together *so as to interlace*, "et font *la haye* les uns parmy les aultres." That is, during each batch of 4 steps, the dancers *change places* one with another, so that if there are three dancers, A, B, C, in the first 4 steps, B and A change places, and make B, A, C; in the next 4 steps, C and A change places, and make B, C, A, etc.

Here is the tune and the formula of steps:

THE HAYE

Beginning at the first complete bar, and reckoning one step to each semibreve: 1. Deux simples (ss). 2. Double (d). 3. ss. 4. d. 5. ss. 6. d. 7. ss. 8. d.

The morisque, which may at all events be compared with the little we know of the Shakespearian morris-dance, seems to have been very violent exercise for the heels (*talons*). Arbeau mentions that it is bad for the gout. The reader will notice that there is a separate movement for each crotchet in the following tune.

MORISQUE

1. Frappe talon droit (strike right heel).
2.   „   gaulche (left).

3. Frappe talon gaulche d.

4.   „   „   g.

5. Frappe talons (perhaps "strike heels together").

6. Soupir (slight pause).

Repeat, then the second half, 1–4, 5–8, 9–12, are same as 1–4, ending with 5, 6, as in the first half.

No wonder it was bad for the gout!

VI

MISCELLANEOUS, INCLUDING PYTHAGOREANISM AND
SHAKESPEARE'S ACCOUNT OF THE MORE SPIRITUAL
SIDE OF MUSIC

A WELL-KNOWN passage in *Twelfth Night* gives us the opinion of Pythagoras "concerning wild-fowl."

The opinion of Pythagoras "concerning music" is at least equally interesting, and is appropriated and assimilated by Shakespeare. The particular branch of the Pythagorean system with which we are concerned, is that which treats of the Music of the Spheres.[1] Besides the two passages here quoted, there are others dealing with this subject, e.g.:

Antony and Cleopatra, V, ii, 84, "the tunèd spheres";
Twelfth Night, III, i, 115, "music from the spheres";
Pericles, V, i, 226, "the music of the spheres."

Thomas Stanley, in his *History of Philosophy*, edition 1701, says:

"This, Pythagoras, first of all the Greeks [560

---

[1] The whole subject of the Music of the Spheres is treated fully in my *Poets and Music* (Dent), pages 121 to 130. The views of authors are traced to the originals, and connections made with Plato, Claudius Ptolemæus, Dante, Chaucer, and others.

B.C.] conceived in his mind; and understood that the spheres sounded something concordant, because of the necessity of proportion, which never forsakes celestial beings." [1]

"Pythagoras, by musical proportion, calleth that a tone, by how much the moon is distant from the earth: from the moon to Mercury the half of that space, and from Mercury to Venus almost as much; from Venus to the sun, sesquiple [i.e. half as much more as a tone]; from the sun to Mars, a tone, that is as far as the moon is from the earth: from Mars to Jupiter, half, and from Jupiter to Saturn, half, and thence to the zodiac, sesquiple." [2]

"Thus there are made *seven tones*, which they call a *diapason* harmony, that is, an *universal concent*, in which Saturn moves in the Doric mood, Jupiter in the Phrygian, and in the rest the like."

"Those sounds which the seven planets, and the sphere of fixed stars, and that which is above us, termed by them Antichthon [opposite the earth], make, Pythagoras affirmed to be the nine Muses; but the composition and symphony . . . he named Mnemosyne [Memory, the mother of the Muses]."

Censorinus, a Roman grammarian, A.D. 238, in his book *De Die Natali*, says:

"To these things we may add what Pythagoras

---

[1] The passage is from Macrobius of the fourth century A.D.
[2] This is from Pliny, the elder, of the first century A.D.

taught, namely, that the whole world was constructed according to musical ratio, and that the seven planets ... have a rhythmical motion and distances adapted to musical intervals, and emit sounds, every one different in proportion to its height [Saturn was said to be the highest, as it is the farthest away, and was supposed to give the gravest note of the heavenly diapason, which note was therefore called *hypate*, or 'highest'], which sounds are so concordant as to produce a most sweet melody, though *inaudible to us by reason of the greatness of the sounds*, which the narrow passages of our ears are not capable of admitting."

These extracts fairly represent the ancient opinion about the music of the spheres. There was a strong tendency not so long ago to revive the notion, and to make an absurd comparison between the law of musical harmonics and Bode's law of the planetary distances. The two sets of numbers have nothing in common. The planetary numbers are 4, 7, 10, 16, 28, 52, 100: whereas the harmonic series in musical sounds is 4, 8, 12, 16, 20, 24, 28! But even Kepler was taken in! see *Poets and Music*, p. 67.

The idea of the musical chorus or dance of the heavenly bodies was perfectly familiar to all writers in the sixteenth and seventeenth centuries. An excellent example is in *Paradise Lost*, Book V, in the twelve lines beginning "So spake the Omnipotent."

Even finer is the thirteenth verse of the *Nativity Hymn*:

> Ring out, ye crystal spheres,
> Once bless our human ears,
> If ye have power to touch our senses so;
> And let your silver chime
> Move in melodious time,
> And let the bass of heaven's deep organ blow;
> And, with your nine-fold harmony,
> Make up full consort to the angelic symphony.

No one could help thinking of the text in Job xxxviii, 7, "When the morning stars sang together," in this connection, and Milton naturally refers to it in the previous verse.

Here follow the two Shakespeare extracts. The second one is full of beauty of every kind, but the Pythagoreanism is in the last six lines, with Shakespeare's own view about *why* we cannot hear the heavenly music.

As You Like It, II, vii, 5:

Duke Senior [*of Jaques*].
    If he, *compact of jars*, grow musical,
    We shall have shortly *discord in the spheres*.

Merchant of Venice, V, i, 51:

Lor. My friend Stephano, signify, I pray you,
    Within the house, your mistress [Portia] is at hand;
    And *bring your music forth into the air.*
                                        [*Exit Stephano.*
[Lorenzo and Jessica alone.]

Lor. How sweet the moonlight sleeps upon this bank!
  Here we will sit, and *let the sounds of music*
  Creep in our ears : soft stillness and the night,
  Become the touches of sweet harmony.

.   .   .   .   .

Line 60:

There 's not the *smallest orb*, which thou behold'st,
But in his motion like an angel sings,
Still *quiring* to the young-ey'd cherubims;
Such harmony is in immortal souls;
But, *whilst this muddy vesture of decay*
Doth grossly close it in, we cannot hear it.[1]

This is finer than Pythagoras.

The next three passages are concerned with the "fantasie" of music. Jaques gives an opinion in a general form, viz. that the musician's "melancholy" is "fantastical"; Mariana and the Duke speak of a certain *doubleness* that may be noticed in the action of music on the mind. Jessica is "never merry" when she hears sweet music; Lorenzo descants on the evident effects of music on even hardened natures; while Portia and Nerissa preach a neat little sermon on the text, "Nothing is good without respect," with musical illustrations of the powerful influence of time and place; e.g. the silence of night makes the music sound sweeter than by day; the crow sings as well as the lark, if the circumstances favour the crow, or if the lark is not present to give immediate

[1] This is from Censorinus (third century A.D.), quoting Pythagoras (sixth century B.C.); see above, p. 148.

comparison; and even the nightingale's song is no better than the wren's, "by day, when every goose is cackling."

As You Like It, IV, i, 13:

Jaques. I have neither the scholar's melancholy, which is emulation; nor the *musician's*, which is *fantastical*, etc.

Measure for Measure, IV, i, 12. Enter Duke, disguised as a friar (after Song).

Mariana. I cry you mercy, sir; and well could wish
    You had not found me here *so musical*:
    Let me excuse me, and believe me so,
    My mirth it much displeas'd, but *pleas'd my woe*.
Duke. 'Tis good: though *music oft hath such a charm*,
    To make bad good, and good provoke to harm.

Merchant of Venice, V, i, 66. Enter musicians.

Lor. Come ho! and wake Diana with a *hymn*:
    With sweetest *touches* pierce your mistress' ear,
    And draw her home *with music*.   [*Music.*
Jessica. I am *never merry when I hear sweet music*.
Lor. The reason is, *your spirits are attentive*.
    For . . . *colts* . . .

       .   .   .   .   .

    If they but hear perchance *a trumpet* sound,
    Or any *air of music touch their ears*,
    You shall perceive them make a *mutual stand*,
    Their savage eyes turn'd to a modest gaze,
    By the sweet power of music: therefore, the poet
    Did feign that Orpheus drew trees, stones, and floods:
    Since nought so stockish, hard, and full of rage,
    But *music for the time doth change his nature*.
    The man that hath no music in himself,

Nor is not mov'd with concord of sweet sounds,
Is fit for treasons, stratagems, and spoils;
The motions of his spirit are dull as night,
And his affections dark as Erebus.
Let no such man be trusted.—Mark the music.

Line 97.   Portia and Nerissa.

Por. . . . Music ! hark !
Ner. It is your music, madam, *of the house.*
Por. Nothing is good, I see, without respect.
   Methinks, *it sounds much sweeter than by day.*
Ner. Silence bestows that virtue on it, madam.
Por. The *crow* doth sing as sweetly as the *lark,*
   When neither is attended; and I think,
   The *nightingale,* if she should sing *by day,*
   When every goose is cackling, *would be thought*
   No better a musician than the wren.
   How many things *by season* season'd are
   To their right praise, and true perfection.

Here is an example of a superstitious meaning
attaching to supposed mysterious music.

There are very few cases of this kind in Shakespeare, i.e. where the music of the stage is an integral
part of the drama.

Antony and Cleopatra, IV, iii, 12.   Music of hautboys under the stage.

4 *Soldier.* . . . Peace, what noise?
1 *Soldier.*   List, list!
2 *Soldier.* Hark!
1 *Soldier.*   Music in the air.
3 *Soldier.*   Under the earth.
4 *Soldier.* It signs well, does it not?

3 *Soldier.*   No.
1 *Soldier.*   Peace, I say!
  What should this mean?
2 *Soldier.* 'Tis the god Hercules, whom Antony lov'd,
  Now leaves him.

A very usual popular amusement was the masque, which would consist of a public procession with decorated cars containing the characters, accompanied by hobby-horses, tumblers, and open-air music.[1] This is referred to in the next passage, where Theseus speaks of the masque as an "abridgement" for the evening, that is, an entertainment to shorten the hours. The lamentable play of Pyramus and Thisbe follows, which, it will be noticed, has some of the main features of a masque.

Midsummer Night's Dream, V, i, 39 :

Theseus. Say, what abridgment have you for this evening?
What masque, what music? . . .

              .   .   .   .

[*Reads from the paper.*]
  "A tedious brief scene of young Pyramus,
  And his love Thisbe; very tragical mirth."
  Merry and tragical! Tedious and brief!
  That is, hot ice, and wonderous strange snow.
  How shall we find the *concord of this discord*?

In the *Merchant of Venice*, Shylock mentions the procession of a masque through the streets, forbidding Jessica to look out of the window at these "Christian

----

[1] Cf. *Don Quixote*, Part II, chap. xx.

fools with varnished faces." The music accompanying the procession is named, viz. drum and fife.

Act II, v, 22:

Lancelot. You shall see a *masque* . . .
Shylock. What! are there *masques*?
                                    Hear you me, Jessica.
Lock up my doors; and *when you hear the drum,*
And the *vile squeaking of the wryneck'd fife,*
Clamber not you up to the casements then,
Nor thrust your head into the public street
To gaze on *Christian fools with varnish'd faces.*

The "vile squeaking of the wryneck'd fife" is of
some musical interest. The adjective "wryneck'd"
refers, not to the instrument itself, which was straight,
but to the player, whose head had to be slightly
twisted round to get at the mouthpiece. Mersennus
(b. 1588) says that the fife is the same as the *tibia
Helvetica*, which was simply a small edition of the
flauto traverso, or German flute. That is, the fife
of those days was much the same as the modern fife
of the cheaper kind, with the usual six holes, and
a big hole near the stopped end, where the breath
was applied. The instrument was therefore held
across (traverso) the face of the player, whose head
would be turned sidewards, and hence comes Shylock's
description of it as the "wryneck'd fife." Much
confusion has been caused by various writers who
have tried to explain *wryneck'd fife.* See Mr.
Christopher Welch's large book, *Lectures on the*

Recorder (Frowde), pp. 240–6.   Here such men as Engel, Knight, and Halliwell are refuted, with no difficulty.   Not only impossible instruments have been suggested, but even the bird (ἴυγξ, wryneck) has been called on.   Shylock's speech is supposed to be an actual imitation of Horace (seventh ode, third book):

> Prima nocte domum claude: neque in vias
> Sub cantu querulæ despice tibiæ.

> First thing at nightfall, lock the doors;
> And when you hear his flute a-squeal,
> Keep your head in.
> (Horace's advice to Asteria.)

In *Much Ado about Nothing*, Benedick draws a distinction between the drum and fife and the tabor and pipe.   The former (see *Othello*, III, iii, 353) were of a decided military cast; whereas the latter were more associated with May Day entertainments, bull-baitings, and out-of-door amusements generally.   The tabor was a little drum, the pipe (as explained before, in Section III, about Autolycus) a whistle with only three holes.   The two were played simultaneously by one person.

Much Ado about Nothing, II, iii, 13.   Benedick, of Claudio in love.

Ben. I have known, when there was no *music* with him but the *drum and the fife*; and now had he rather hear the *tabor and the pipe*: . . . but till all graces be in one woman, one woman shall not come in my grace. Rich she shall be, that 's certain; wise, or I 'll none; . . . of good discourse, an *excellent musician,* and her hair shall be of what colour it please God.

Besides these more civilised "pipes," the country-man's pipe of corn-stalk is mentioned by Titania, in *Midsummer Night's Dream,* II, ii, 8. This was really a "reed," not a whistle of any kind.

The tabor leads one on to the tabourine, which was the full-sized military drum, corresponding to the modern side-drum. See *Troilus and Cressida,* IV, v, 275, "Beat loud the tabourines," and *Antony and Cleopatra,* IV, viii, 37, "our rattling tabourines."

The drum supplied the great proportion of military music in those days, besides having its importance as a means of signalling orders to the troops. This is dealt with more fully in the section below on Stage Directions.

Parolles' sham anxiety about a lost drum is mentioned fourteen or fifteen times in *All 's Well that Ends Well,* III, v, and vi; and IV, i. Parolles earns his nickname of "Tom Drum" in Act V, iii, 320.

The following is an interesting passage of a more serious kind.

King John, V, ii, 164:

Lewis [Dauphin].
    Strike up the *drums!* and let the tongue of war
    Plead for our interest, and our being here.
Bastard. Indeed, your *drums,* being *beaten,* will cry out;

And so shall you, being *beaten*.   Do but start
An *echo* with the clamour of thy drum,
And even at hand a *drum* is ready *brac'd*,
That shall reverberate all as loud as thine;
Sound but *another*, and another shall,
As loud as thine, *rattle the welkin's ear*,
And mock the deep-mouth'd thunder.

An entirely different use of the drum is alluded
to by Parolles, in his slanderous evidence against
Captain Dumain.

All's Well that Ends Well, IV, iii, 262:

1 *Soldier*. What say you to his expertness in war?
Parolles. 'Faith, sir, he has *led the drum before the English
tragedians*, ... and more of his soldiership I know not.

There are several occasions in Shakespeare when
trumpets are sounded to herald the approach of play-
actors, but *drums* are not mentioned in this connection except here.[1]   Rimbault's Preface to Purcell's
opera *Bonduca* (Musical Antiquarian Society) says
that a play was always introduced by the trumpet
sounding three times, after which the Prologue
entered.   Dekker, referring to the list of *errata* in
his *Satiromastix*, 1602, says: "Instead of the trumpets
sounding thrice before the play begin, it shall not be
amiss for him that will read, first to behold this short
Comedy of Errors."

[1] See *Don Quixote*, Part II, chap. xxvi, where the puppet-show
performance opens with a flourish from a number of "atabeles
[kettle-drums] y trompetas" and the discharge of "mucha artilleria."

VII

*With references to the same Words as they occur
in the Text*

Alarum, Alarums (of drums), occurs as a stage direction about seventy-two times in fourteen of the historical plays, always in connection with battle. It is found alone, as above, about forty-five times, sometimes qualified, e.g. *Loud alarum, Low alarum, Short alarum, Alarum within. Alarum and Excursions* occurs about twenty-one times, always in fight. ("Excursions" merely means "parties of men running about"; see the stage direction, 1 *Henry VI*, IV, vi: "Excursions, *wherein* Talbot's son is hemmed about"; also ibid., I, v, where the direction has "Alarum. *Skirmishings*," instead of the usual "Excursions.")

A few special cases are: "Alarum *with thunder and lightning*," 1 *Henry VI*, I, iv, 97; "*Flourish and Alarums*," used by Richard III to drown the reproaches of Queen Elizabeth, etc.; "Alarum and *chambers* [cannon] *go off*," *Henry V*, Act III, line 33 of the chorus, and again ibid., end of scene i; "Alarum *and cry within*, 'Fly, fly, fly,'" *Julius Cæsar*, V, v, 41;

"Alarum afar off, *as at a sea fight*," *Antony and Cleopatra*, IV, x.

Out of the seventy-two cases in the stage directions, seventy mean a call to battle by *drums*. The two exceptions are 2 *Henry VI*, II, iii, 92, and *Troilus and Cressida*, IV, v, 12, 117, where the alarum is identified with trumpets.

Skeat gives the original of the term as "all' arme" (Italian), a war cry of the time of the Crusades. For the *form* of the word, he compares *arum* (arm) and *koren* (corn).

"*Alarum*" in the text

The word is used thirteen times in the text of Shakespeare; and in six of these it refers to *drums*, as in the stage directions, 1 *Henry VI*, I, ii, 18, iv, 99, II, i, 42; *Richard III*, I, i, 7; *Coriolanus*, II, ii, 76; *Henry V*, IV, vi, 35.

But in two of the remaining examples, alarum is distinctly said to be *trumpets*, 2 *Henry VI*, II, iii, 93, and V, ii, 3; while other more extended meanings are found, e.g. in *Venus and Adonis*, line 700, where it refers to the noise of the dogs hunting the hare; in *Macbeth*, II, iii, 75, and V, v, 51, where alarum is used of a bell; also in *Lucrece*, 433, of Tarquin's "drumming heart" "giving the hot charge," and *Othello*, II, iii, 27, of Desdemona's voice, which Iago says is "an alarum to love."

Flourish, either simply in this form, or "Flourish of

trumpets" (six times), or "Flourish of cornets" (twice), occurs about sixty-eight times in seventeen plays.

Out of these, it is used some twenty-two times for the entrance or exit of a king or queen; twelve times for the entrance or exit of a distinguished person not a king; ten times in the public welcome of a queen or great general; seven times it marks the end of a scene; six times heralds a victorious force; twice announces the proclamation of a king; twice signalizes the entrance or exit of senate or tribunes; and twice gives warning of the approach of play-actors (see Section VI, at end), or the commencement of a play (Players in *Hamlet*, and Pyramus and Thisbe in *Midsummer Night's Dream*).

Some solitary uses are where Richard III orders a flourish to drown the reproaches of Queen Elizabeth and the Duchess of York; the occasion of the betrothal of Henry V and Katherine of France; and the public welcome of the three Ladies in *Coriolanus*. The last is *A Flourish with drums and trumpets*, which occurs several times. In Grove's *Dictionary*, ed. 1890 (under "Fanfare"), is given a seven-bar flourish which is believed to be of Charles II's time, and is still used at the opening of Parliament. (Appendix.)

"Flourish" in the text is only found twice. In *Richard III*, IV, iv, 149, "A flourish, trumpets!—strike alarum, drums!" we have a clear definition of the two terms mentioned; and in *Merchant of Venice*,

III, ii, 49, "Even as the flourish when true subjects bow To a new-crowned monarch," a reference to the principal use of the flourish, which was to signify the presence of royal persons.

Trumpets, A trumpet sounds, Trumpet sounded within, Drums and trumpets, Flourish of trumpets (six times).

One or other of the above occurs some fifty-one times in twenty-two plays, either alone, or in connection with sennet, discharge of cannon, etc. On eighteen of these occasions it announces the entrance or presence of a king or royal personage; thirteen times it figures as part of the proceedings in duels; ten times signifies the entrance or exit of principal persons, not royal, great generals, etc.; three times precedes a public procession, with royal persons in it; twice it is connected with the advent of royal heralds; and once with the arrival of players (*Taming of the Shrew*, Prologue. See also Flourish).

Thus "Trumpets" divides the honours with "Flourish" as the mark of royalty.

Examples of the use of the term in the text are numerous, and are found in most of the plays. They are not generally of very special interest.

Music, Music plays, Music within.

This direction is found forty-one times in twenty-two plays, half of which are comedies.

In eight cases we have *Music* during a speech or

dream of one of the characters; seven times as the symphony or the accompaniment to a song; seven times in wedding processions or pageants; six times for dancing; and five times during a banquet.

To give a just idea of the amount of stage music considered necessary in or near Shakespeare's time, there must be added to the above, all the stage directions in other terms, e.g. *Hautboys*, which is found about fourteen times.

Here are a few relics of stage music before Shakespeare's day.

The playing of the minstrels is frequently mentioned in the old Miracle Plays, and the instruments used were the horn, pipe, tabret, and flute. In the Prologue to the Miracle Play, Childermas Day, 1512, the minstrels are requested to "do their diligence," and at the end of the play to "geve us a daunce."

In Richard Edwards's *Damon and Pythias*, acted in 1565, there is a stage direction: "Here Pythias sings and the regalles play." Also, when Pythias is carried to prison, "the regalls play a mourning song." Thus the regal,[1] a tiny organ that could be easily

---

[1] The regal was made in two forms, one with beating reeds, the other with ordinary wood organ pipes. The latter was a good size with four octaves compass, and stood on a frame with its own legs: the former was often made in the shape of a large book, hence it got the name "Bible regal." When the "book" was opened, the covers proved to be a pair of bellows. See Galpin's *Old English Instruments of Music* (Methuen), pp. 230 and 232, where pictures of seventeenth-century regals are given.

carried about, was considered a proper instrument for the stage.   In the old comedy, *Gammer Gurton's Needle*, 1566, mention is made by one of the characters of the music between the acts:

Into the town will I, my friendes to visit there,
And hither straight again to see the end of this gere;
In the meantime, fellows, pype up your fidles: I say take them,
And let your friends hear such mirth as ye can make them.

In Gascoigne's *Jocasta*, 1566, each act is preceded by a dumb show, accompanied by "viols, cythren, bandores, flutes, cornets, trumpets, drums, fifes, and still-pipes."   In Anthony Munday's comedy *The Two Italian Gentlemen* (about 1584), the different kinds of music to be played after each act are mentioned e.g. "a pleasant galliard," "a solemn dump," or "a pleasant allemayne."   A little later, Marston, in his *Sophonisba*, 1606, goes into considerable detail as to the music between the Acts; after Act I, "the cornets and organs playing loud full music"; after Act II, "organs mixed with recorders"; after Act III, "organs, viols, and voices"; after Act IV, "a base lute and a treble viol"; and in the course of Act V, "infernall music plays softly."   Fiddles, flutes, and hautboys are mentioned by other dramatists as instruments in use at the theatre at this time.[1]

[1] Campion's masque (Lord Hayes), given at Whitehall in 1607, may illustrate the use of music on the stage at this period.   The King's entrance was marked by a band of "hoboys" (probably six

Rimbault's Introduction to Purcell's opera *Bonduca* gives the names of twenty-six masques and plays produced between 1586 and 1642 (when the theatres were closed), all of which contained important music. Amongst them are *Jane Shore*, by Henry Lacy, 1586, with music by William Byrd; seven masques by Ben Jonson, dating 1605–21, four of which had music by Ferrabosco; a masque by Beaumont (1612) with music by Coperario; a play, *Valentinian*, by Beaumont and Fletcher (1617), set by Robert Johnson; *The Triumphs of Peace*, by Shirley (1633), with music by William Lawes and Simon Ives; several other masques, set by Henry Lawes, who did the music to Milton's *Comus* (1634), etc. The list also includes Shakespeare's *Tempest*, with Robert Johnson's music, two numbers of which, viz. "Full fathom five," and "Where the bee sucks," are printed in Bridge's *Shakespeare Songs*, with date 1612.

Retreat, or *A Retreat sounded*, generally with Alarum, or Excursions, or with both.

of them, playing a march), placed in a wood at top of the hill. Then, when His Majesty and his "trayne" were seated, the "consort" began to play. There were ten of these "consort" players, including two sizes of lutes, a bandora (again a sort of lute), a double sackbott (i.e. a trombone), a harpsichord, and two treble violins: on the other side were nine violins, and three lutes, and *to answer both the consorts* (as it were in a triangle), six cornets, and six "chappell" voices, etc In the first scene, also, four "silvans" sang, and accompanied themselves on four lutes (one a bandora) while flowers were being "strown about."

Retreat by itself occurs only three times, but in company with Alarums and (or) Excursions may be found in sixteen other places. The whole nineteen cases occur in eleven plays.

The word explains itself. The actual notes of a retreat of Shakespeare's time are not known.

In the text it has the same meaning.

1 *Henry VI*, II, ii, 3. "Here sound retreat, and cease our hot pursuit."

2 *Henry VI*, IV, viii, 4. "Dare any be so bold to sound retreat or parley, when I command them kill?"

1 *Henry IV*, V, iv, 159. "The trumpet sounds retreat; the day is ours."

Henry V, III, ii, 89. "*Macmorris.* The work ish give over, the trumpet sound the retreat."

March, Dead march.

There are eighteen marches provided for altogether; four are dead marches; three national, viz. English, French, and Danish[1]; and eleven ordinary military marches.

Probably all are identified with *Drums*, without any other instruments. For the three national marches, see 1 *Henry VI*, III, 30, 33; and *Hamlet*, III, ii, 91.

Hawkins gives (*History of Music*, p. 229) the text of a Royal Warrant of Charles I, ordering the revival

---

[1] See my *Shakespeare Music* (Curwen) for the music of the "Hamburgh" March, p. 30 ff., taken from the tablature of the Cambridge Lute MS., Dd. ii, 11.

of the ancient "march of this our English nation, so famous in all the honourable achievements and glorious wars of this our kingdome in forraigne parts (being by the approbation of strangers themselves confest and acknowledged the best of all marches)." The warrant goes on to say that this ancient war march of England "was, through the negligence and carelessness of drummers, and by long discontinuance, so altered and changed from the ancient gravitie and majestie thereof, as it was in danger utterly to have bene lost and forgotten." It appears that "our late deare brother prince Henry" had taken steps to have the old march restored, at Greenwich, in 1610; "In confirmation whereof" the warrant orders all English or Welsh drummers to "observe the same," whether at home or abroad, "without any addition or alteration whatever." "Given at our palace of Westminster, the seventh day of February, in the seventh yeare of our raigne, of England, Scotland, France, and Ireland."

Then follows the march, expressed both in musical notes and onomatopoetic words. It consists of a voluntary, and then seven lines of "The March," each of which ends with a "pause." The first line is given thus: "Pou tou pou tou poûng." The next three lines are very similar. Line 5 is more elaborate, and the last two lines run as follows:

"*R R R R* poûng."

"*R R R* pou *R R* pou tou pou *R* tou pou *R* poûng potang."

See the Appendix for the translation into musical notes, which is given in the warrant itself, but the accuracy of which is questionable.

It seems pretty clear that this ancient march of England is of a period long anterior to the warrant of Charles I. Several passages of that document point to this. At any rate, it was so old as to have almost dropped out of knowledge in 1610. See my *Shakespeare Music* (Curwen), p. 41, where suggestions for its use in *Hamlet* are given. Also p. 31, the Hamburgh March.

Hawkins gives an interesting note, in which he mentions that the characteristic of the old English march of the foot was "dignity and gravity," in which it differed greatly from that of the French, which is given by Mersennus (b. 1588) as "brisk and alert."

There is a curious story of a conversation between Marshal Biron, a French general, and Sir Roger Williams, a gallant Low-country soldier of Elizabeth's time. The marshal observed that the English march, *being beaten by the drum*, was slow, heavy, and sluggish. "That may be true," answered Sir Roger, "but slow as it is, it has traversed your master's country from one end to the other."

The references in Shakespeare all go to confirm the

opinion that the march was played by drums alone, e.g. 3 *Henry VI*, I, ii, 69, where the stage direction is "*A march afar off*," which is immediately followed by "I hear their *drums*." Again, in the same play, Act IV, scene vii, line 50, "*Drummer*, strike up, and let us *march* away. [*A march begun*.]"

Hautboys. This is an important musical term, and occurs about fourteen times in eight plays. It always implies a certain special importance in the music, and is generally connected with a royal banquet, masque, or procession. In six cases, at least, the direction has some special qualification, e.g. "Hautboys playing *loud* music"; "*A lofty strain or two* to the hautboys"; "Trumpets and hautboys sounded, and drums beaten *all together*." In *Antony and Cleopatra*, IV, iii, 12, hautboys supply the supposed ominous "music in the air."

The term is closely connected with "Music," the remarks on which apply equally to the present case. (See above, on "Music," and the music of sixteenth-century plays.)

Not long after Shakespeare's time, orchestral music for the theatre consisted of stringed instruments only (i.e. the violin family, violins, violas, violoncellos, and the sole surviving "viol," the double-bass) with harpsichord, for general use; while in the more important pieces, hautboys, and sometimes flutes as well, were added, playing, as a rule, with the first and second violin parts.   This, at any rate, is the case in Purcell's operas.   (Purcell died 1695.)   Thus the word haut-boys represented very nearly the climax of power to seventeenth-century ears.   Anything beyond this was supplied by the addition of trumpets, though this was rare; while drums were very occasionally used.

The stage direction in Shakespeare should not be taken to mean: "Let the hautboys be added to the usual band of strings."   The hautboys were used as a separate family of instruments; there might be four, five, or six, of different sizes, playing as an independent "band," the same applied to "cornets," and to "recorders."   In the last of the above examples *Coriolanus*, V, iv, 50, we have the extreme limit of power of this time provided for, viz., trumpets *and* hautboys *and* drums, *all together*.   It is interesting to notice the wording of Menenius's description of this stage music: "The trumpets, sackbuts, psalteries, and fifes, Tabors and cymbals."   The "sackbut" was merely our modern slide trombone, while the rest of these instruments were in common use in the sixteenth century, except the psaltery,[1] which Kircher (b. 1601) says is the same as the *nebel* of the Bible.   The picture he gives is remarkably like the dulcimers which may be seen and heard outside public-houses

---

[1] But see *Don Quixote*, Part II, chap. xix, where "salterios" are mentioned in a list of rustic instruments, along with flutes, shepherds' pipes, etc.

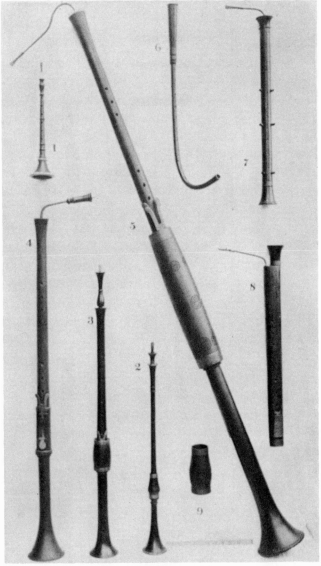

HAUTBOYS (SHAWMS)　　　(See page 170)
(From Canon Galpin's "Old English Instruments of Music")
Nos. 2–5 is a set, early seventeenth century. No. 6 is a krummhorn
(cromorne). Nos. 7 and 8 are "curtals" (cortaut)

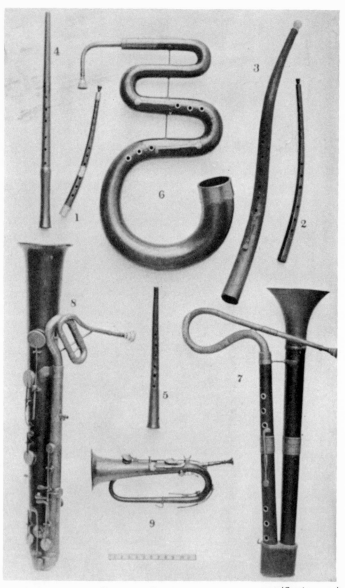

CORNETS, SERPENT, ETC. (*See page* 173)

(*From Canon Galpin's "Old English Instruments of Music"*)

These are all of the cornetto family. The ones Shakespeare would know best
are Nos. 1–5. All are now obsolete.

to this very day, i.e. a small hollow chest, with the strings stretched across it. An instrument of this kind could be played with the fingers, like a harp, or with a plectrum, like a zither, or with two little knob-sticks, like the dulcimer. Mersennus (b. 1588) also identifies the psaltery with the dulcimer.

In the text, the hautboy is only named once, in 2 *Henry IV*, III, ii, 332, near the end of Falstaff's soliloquy, on old men and lying, where he says that Shallow was such a withered little wretch that *the case of a treble hautboy* was a mansion for him, a court.

The "treble" hautboy corresponds with our modern instrument, and was the smallest in size of the hautboy tribe, of which only two now survive, viz. the oboe proper, and its cousin, which is a fifth lower in pitch, and correspondingly larger, and which has curiously picked up the name of corno inglese, cor anglais, or English horn. This is a "ghost" word. "Anglais" is a blunder for "anglé," because the tube was bent.[1] None the less it is the alto hautboy. The tenor and bass of the family have not survived. Hautboys in four parts were the backbone of the French regimental bands in Lully's time, i.e. about 1670. (Appendix.)

The spelling of the word in the old editions of

---

[1] A similar blunder happened to "Krummhorn," which was bent like a hockey club (*krumm* is German for crooked). It was used as a name for an organ stop, and then corrupted to "Cremona" and supposed to be an imitation of a violin (!).

Shakespeare is "hoeboy," which is very like the modern German *hoboe*.

Sennet. This is a rare direction, and is found only nine times in eight plays, as against sixty-eight "flourishes" and fifty-one "trumpets." The notes of a sennet are unknown. Three times it marks the entrance or exit of a Parliament, three times is used in a royal or quasi-royal procession, and the remaining cases are royal, or near it.

In the first folio of *Henry V*, the word is spelt *senet*, but in later ones, *sonet*, as if the former were a misprint. In Marlowe's *Faustus* (published 1604), Act III, scene i, we find *"Sound a sonnet"* [enter Pope, Cardinal, etc.]. Also the French cavalry of 1636 used trumpet calls named *sonneries*. These seem to point to a derivation of the word from *sonare*, and thus the spelling ought to be *sonnet*, not *sennet*.

But other forms are found—*synnet, signet, signate*, which may be proper derivatives of *signum*, and thus make this trumpet call "a signal," instead of "a sounding"; or (which is as likely) may be corruptions, perhaps of the somewhat featureless form "synnet," caused by a misunderstanding of the original misspelling "senet."

In the text of Shakespeare the word does not occur.

Cornets, or *Flourish cornets* (only twice).

This is also rare, occurring only eight times in

four plays. One case only is in war, the others being all connected with royal or triumphal processions.

The term is by no means synonymous with trumpets. The cornet was an entirely different instrument, and the use of it accordingly is very much more limited in these stage directions. It was a sort of horn (hence its name), with a cup mouthpiece, and finger holes for the intermediate notes of the scale. Hawkins gives pictures of a treble, a tenor, and a bass cornet, copied from Mersennus, who remarks that the sounds of the cornet are vehement, *but* that those who are skilful, such as Quiclet, the royal cornetist (i.e. of France, 1648), are able so to soften and moderate them, that nothing can be more sweet.[1]

Few people now living will remember the serpent, a large, black, curly instrument, of thin wood covered with leather, which helped to play the loud bass in oratorios up to the middle of last century. This serpent was a true cornet in every respect. It may now commonly be seen in exhibitions, museums, and curiosity shops, for it has been entirely superseded by the bass tuba and the euphonium.

In the text the word cornet occurs only once, and in a special sense; see 1 *Henry VI*, IV, iii, 25, where

[1] See Galpin's illustration, shewing five sizes of cornets as Shakespeare knew them.

Richard Duke of York accuses Somerset of treachery, and exclaims, "He doth stop my cornets," which simply means "prevents the victory being mine." "Cornets" meant what a "brass band" means to us.

Tucket. Rare, only *seven* times in six different plays. This is one of the several trumpet calls we have noticed. It seems to have been a French term, *toquet,* or *doquet,* and this is defined by Littré as "quatrième partie de trompette d'une fanfare de cavalerie"—that is, the name "toquet" was applied to the fourth trumpet in a cavalry fanfare. Mr. Aldis Wright, in his Clarendon Press edition of *Henry V,* gives a reference to Markham, quoted by Grose in *Military Antiquities,* which explains "Tucket" as a trumpet signal, which, "being heard simply of itself without addition, commands nothing but *marching after the leader."* Certainly in Shakespeare it seems to be used as a *personal* trumpet call, e.g. *Merchant of Venice,* V, i, 121, Lorenzo says to Portia, "Your husband is at hand; I hear his trumpet," i.e. the "tucket sounded" which is indicated in the stage direction. Other cases of the use of the tucket are quite similar—for instance, the return of Bertram, Count of Rousillon, from war; the arrival of Goneril ("*Cornwall.* What trumpet's that? *Regan.* I know 't, my sister's"); or the embassy of Æneas. Once it is used to herald Cupid and the masked

Amazons, in *Timon of Athens*; and twice at the entrance of Montjoy, the French herald, in *Henry V*.

The connection of the word with *toccare*, *tocco di campana*, *tocsin*, and *Tusch*, has already been explained in the notes on Hortensio's music lesson to Bianca. (See Section II.)

In the Appendix is given an Italian tucket of 1638, and a French one of 1643.

In the text the word is only found once, viz. *Henry V*, IV, ii, 35, where the Constable of France orders the trumpets to "sound the tucket-sonance, and the note to mount," which fits in with Markham's definition, for the passage appears to recognise the tucket as in some sort a *preparatory* signal.

It is perhaps worth noting, that of the seven tuckets in the stage directions, only one, Goneril's, is supposed to be an English one. In the single instance just given of its use in the text, it is a *French* general who uses the word. Perhaps this may be regarded as confirming the view of its foreign origin.

Parley, or *Trumpets sound a parley*, either alone, or with *Retreat*. This call is named in the stage directions seven times in five plays, viz., 1 *Henry VI*, *three times*; 2 *Henry VI*, once; *Richard II*, once; 1 *Henry IV*, once; and *Henry V*, once. It means either a trumpet call announcing an *embassy* from one party to the other, or for *cessation* of hostilities during the fight itself. Of course the name is derived from *parler*, with a reference to the proposed "pow-wow" of the opposing forces.

The notes of a parley do not appear to exist.

Perhaps a little light may be got out of the symphony to Purcell's duet in *King Arthur*, "Sound a parley, ye fair," the first notes of which, as for a trumpet in C, are:

In the text, the word is used several times. In three cases, *John*, II, 205, 226, and *Henry V*, III, iii, 2, "the parle" means the conference of the parties itself, not the trumpet call summoning them. In the rest, "parle" or "parley" simply means the sound of the trumpet, as explained above. *2 Henry VI*, IV, viii, 4; *Richard II*, I,ˑi, 192, III, iii, 33; *3 Henry VI*, V, i, 16; *Othello*, II, iii, 23.

Horns, or *Horns wind a peal*, or *Horns winded*.

This is very rare. Seven times in only four plays, one of which is the doubtful *Titus Andronicus*.

Three times it is used of hunting horns, *Titus Andronicus*, II, ii, at beginning and line 10, and in the Induction of the *Taming of the Shrew*; twice as a part of Lear's lessened state, *Lear*, I, iii and iv; once announcing the Post from England, *3 Henry VI*, III, iii; and once blown by Talbot as a military signal at the forcing of Auvergne Castle gates, 1 *Henry VI*, II, iii.

The "peal" of horns referred to in *Titus Andronicus*, II, ii, 10, is a technical term in forestry for a particular set of notes on the horn. Méhul (1763–1817), in the overture to his opera *Le Jeune Henri*, introduces several old French hunting fanfares, which perhaps may give an idea of what was meant by "Horns wind a peal." (See Appendix.) Also in Purcell's *Dido and Æneas*, No. 16 (date 1689[1]), in the scene between the Sorceress and the two witches who are plotting the destruction of "Elissa," at the words "Hark! the cry comes on apace," the violins give an imitation of a hunting call.

The only instance of the use of the word "peal" in the text is in the same passage, *Titus Andronicus*, II, ii, 5, where Titus tells his hunters to "ring a hunter's peal." Here we have a last example of punning on a technical term of music.

[1] So the latest authority, Mr. Barclay Squire. The *Oxford History of Music* gives the date 1680.

APPENDIX

1. Example of Descant (*Lucrece*, 1134) from Morley, 1597.
See pp. 5 and 24.

If the lower part was added extempore, it was called
descant, but if written down as here, it was called prick-
song, because "pricked" down. The plain-song is perhaps
more often found in a lower part, the descant being higher.
From the position of the added part, the above example is
called "bass" descant.

2. Divisions on a Ground Bass for viol-da-gamba, by
Christopher Sympson, 1665. See p. 27, *Romeo and Juliet*,
III, v, 25.

The "Ground" itself is in large notes, the necessary chords
(which were *never* written down) are indicated in small notes.
This the organist or harpsichordist plays again and again,
as often as necessary.

Here is a division for the viol, such as the player would
produce extempore, with the above Ground before him.

179

Division No. 1

Division No. 3 (more elaborate).

3. Example of Sol-fa, sixteenth and seventeenth centuries. See p. 35, *King Lear*, I, ii, 137.

Fa sol la fa sol la MI fa   fa sol la fa sol la MI fa

The augmented fourths formed by the notes fa and mi, marked with ×, are the *mi contra fa*, which *diabolus est*, or "is the *divider*" (see p. 36).

Solmization of the six notes of the Hexachord, eleventh century. See p. 38, *Taming of the Shrew*, III, i, 72.

(Natural Hexachord)   (Hard Hexachord)

Ut   Re   Mi   Fa   Sol   La   Ut   Re   Mi   Fa   Sol   La

The six notes from F, with B *flat*, were called the "Soft" Hexachord.

4. Lesson for the lute, by Thomas Mace (b. 1613) from *Musick's Monument*, 1676. See p. 58, *Taming of the Shrew*, III, i, 58.

"My Mistress."

Cf. p. 30, on "broken" music.

5. Tune of "Light o' Love," original words not known, but date before 1570. See p. 69, *Much Ado about Nothing*, V, iv, 41, etc.

6. Parson Hugh's song, "To Shallow Rivers," tune anonymous, date probably sixteenth century. See p. 69, *Merry Wives of Windsor*, III, i, 18.

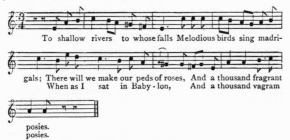

This poor tune is certainly no more than a corrupt form of

"Walsingham." The right tune is that to "Come live with me," No. 7.

7. "Come live with me," tune printed 1612, but probably much older. See p. 70, Marlowe's *Passionate Shepherd*, *Merry Wives of Windsor*, III, i, 18.

Come live with me, and be my love,   And we will all the pleasures prove,

That hills and valleys, dales and fields, And all the craggy mountain yields.
By shallow rivers,   to whose falls melodious birds sing madrigals.

8. Peg-a-Ramsey. See p. 70, *Twelfth Night*, II, iii, 76.

Sir Toby

9. "Three merry men be we." See p. 71, *Twelfth Night*, II, iii, 70.
Words from Peele's *Old Wives' Tale*, 1595, where it is sung. Music from J. Playford, *c.* 1650, but may be older.

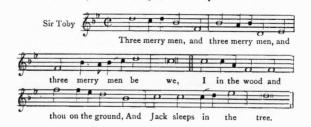

Sir Toby

Three merry men, and three merry men, and

three merry men be   we,   I in the wood and

thou on the ground, And Jack sleeps in   the   tree.

10. "There dwelt a man in Babylon." See p. 70, *Twelfth Night*, II, iii, 80. It is merely a corrupt form of "Green

Sleeves." The correct version (see No. 19) fits the words quite well.

Here is one verse of the "Ballad of Constant Susanna," to which Toby refers.

> There dwelt a man in Babylon
> Of reputation great by fame;
> He took to wife a faire woman,
> Susanna she was callde by name.
> A woman faire and vertuous,
>   Lady, lady!
> Why should we not of her learn thus
>   To live godly?

11. "Farewell dear heart." See p. 70, *Twelfth Night*, II, iii, 102. This is by Robert Jones, published 1600, a four-part song with lute accompaniment; see my *Shakespeare Music* (Curwen, 1912), p. 23. Here is the air:

12. "Hey Robin." *Twelfth Night*, IV, ii. This is pre-Shakespearian, both words and music. See the complete thing in my (Curwen) book named above, p. 25. The Clown is just quoting the first phrases of a round for three (or four) voices. See British Museum, add. MS. 31922, folio 54.

For the rest of the words of "A Robyn, Jolly Robyn," see Percy's *Reliques*, vol. i, p. 132.

13. "Whoop, do me no harm, good man." See p. 71, *Winter's Tale*, IV, iii, 198. The rest of the words are in Gibbon, p. 104: "The sweet pretty Jinny sat on a hill," but several ballads printed in the latter part of the sixteenth century go to this tune:

14. Stephano's "scurvy tunes," *Tempest*, II, ii, 41 (see p. 71). "As sung by Mr. Bannister"(1667).

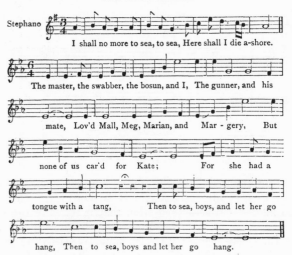

Stephano

I shall no more to sea, to sea, Here shall I die a-shore.

The master, the swabber, the bosun, and I, The gunner, and his

mate, Lov'd Mall, Meg, Marian, and Mar - gery, But

none of us car'd for Kate; For she had a

tongue with a tang, Then to sea, boys, and let her go

hang, Then to sea, boys and let her go hang.

15. "Jog On." See p. 71, *Winter's Tale*, IV, ii, 125. Two more stanzas were first printed 1661, see Chappell, vol. i, p. 160. The tune is in the Fitzwilliam Virginal Book (Queen Elizabeth's Virginal Book), where it has the name

Hanskin.

Autolycus

Jog on, jog on, the foot-path way, And merrily hent the

stile - a: A mer - ry heart goes all the day, Your sad tires

in a mile - - a.

16. "The hunt is up." See p. 72, *Romeo and Juliet*, III, v, 34. The tune is at least as old as 1537, when John Hogon

was proceeded against for singing it with certain political
words.

The hunt is up, the hunt is up, and it is well-nigh day; And Harry our king is gone hunt-ing to bring his deer to lay.

Grove (see under Ballad) gives quite another tune, to which
"Chevy Chase" also was sung. It is, however, sufficiently
like to make possible a suggestion that it is really the same
tune.

The tune here printed was also sung (1584) to "O sweete
Olyver, leave me not behind the," but altered to four in a
bar. See *As You Like It*, III, iii, 95, where a verse is given
which will easily fit to the music.

17. "Heart's Ease." See p. 72, *Romeo and Juliet*, IV, v,
100. Words not known. Tune before 1560.

Gibbon (p. 46) gives another "Heart's Ease," "Sing care
away with sport and play." The tune given here is that of
the Cambridge Lute Book, Dd. ii, 11, for which see the

photograph on p. x of my *Shakespeare Music* (Curwen). No words are given, but the name *Hartes eafe* is written in the usual place, viz. the *end* of the music.

18. "Where griping grief." See p. 72, *Romeo and Juliet*, IV, v, 125. By Richard Edwards, poet and composer (d. 1566).

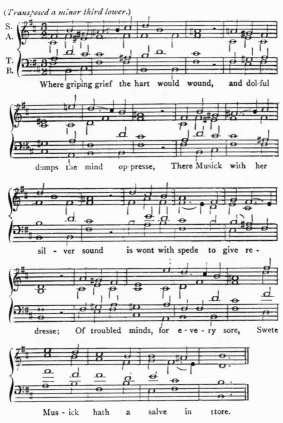

(Transposed a minor third lower.)

Where griping grief the hart would wound, and dol-ful domps the mind op-presse, There Musick with her sil - ver sound is wont with spede to give re - dresse; Of troubled minds, for e - ve - ry sore, Swete Mus - ick hath a salve in store.

19. "Green Sleeves." See p. 73, *Merry Wives of Windsor*, II, i, 60, etc. The tune is probably of Henry VIII's time.

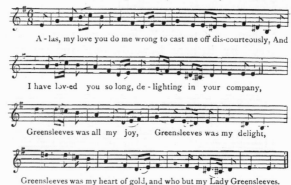

A - las, my love you do me wrong to cast me off dis-courteously, And

I have lov-ed you so long, de - lighting in your company,

Greensleeves was all my joy, Greensleeves was my delight,

Greensleeves was my heart of gold, and who but my Lady Greensleeves.

20. "Carman's Whistle." See p. 74, 2 *Henry IV*, III, ii, 320. Tune as given by Byrd, who wrote variations on it before 1591.

21. "Fortune my foe." See p. 75, *Merry Wives of Windsor*, III, iii, 62. This old tune is, at latest, of Elizabeth's day, and most likely much older. The words here set are given in Burney, and the harmony is by Byrd, who wrote variations on it which appear in the *Fitzwilliam Virginal Book*. "Fortune my foe" is not the only popular tune of old days which lived on as a hymn tune. It appears with Robert Jones's "Fare-

well, dear heart," in a Dutch hymn book published at Amster-
dam in 1713 (Kamphuysen). Jones's music is fitted to
"Heilgierig mensch," and "Fortune" to a metrical version of
Psalm 129, "Zy hebben my (zoo zegge Israel)."

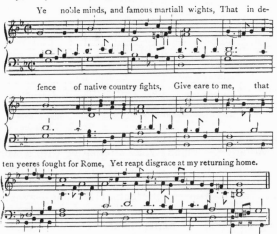

The above words are the first verse of "Titus Andronicus's
Complaint," which Burney says was originally written to this
tune. The ballad is given in full in Percy's *Reliques*, vol. i,
p. 180.

22. Ophelia's songs. See p. 75, *Hamlet*, IV, v.

I.

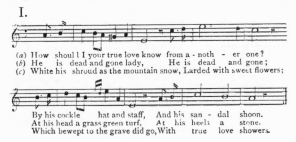

This is a striking example of corruption by stage use. It is a badly damaged version of "Walsingham," given by Bull and Byrd in the *Fitzwilliam Virginal Book*. See Dowland's setting of "Walsingham" for lute, p. 59.

IA.

As yee came ffrom the hol-y land Of — Wal-sing - ham
How shold I know your true love,that have mett many a one

Mett you not with my true love by the way as you came?
As I came ffrom the ho - ly land,that have come that have gone?

The dialogue form of the poem is charmingly indicated in Byrd's variations—a man's voice alternating with a woman's. See my book (Curwen), pp. 35–8, for "Walsingham." Walsingham was the celebrated shrine of Our Lady, very popular with pilgrims from Henry III's time (say 1240) to the Dissolution in 1538. The words of the song are by Thomas Deloney, a contemporary of Shakespeare. See Percy's *Reliques*, vol. ii, p. 75.

Erasmus visited Walsingham in 1511, with a young gentleman who afterwards became Bishop Aldrich of Carlisle.

The date of the next is not certain, though probably it is of Shakespeare's time.

II.

(*a*) Good morrow, 'tis St Valentine's day All in the morn betime, And
(*b*) For bonny sweet Robin is all my joy.

I a maid at your window To be your Valen - tine.

The next two are of the same period as I.

III.

They bore him bare-faste on the bier ; And in his grave rain'd many a tear.

"Walsingham" again!

IV.

(a) And will he not come a - gain - - ? And will he not come a -
(b) His beard as white as snow, All flax - en was his

gain - - ? No, no, he is dead. Go to thy death bed : He
poll ; He's gone, he's gone, And we cast away moan ; God ha'

ne-ver will come a - gain - - -.
mer - cy on his soul!

Line 184, "Bonny Sweet Robin." With the exception of this one line, and the title, "My Robin is to the greenwood gone," nothing remains of this song, but the following tune, which is of some date before 1597.

V.

My Robin is to the greenwood gone.

For

bonny sweet Robin is all my joy.

23. Catches, of sixteenth century, probably long anterior to Shakespeare.

I. "Hold thy peace." See p. 76, *Twelfth Night*, II, iii. For *three* voices, Sir Toby, Sir Andrew, and Feste the clown, who begins the catch. The second man follows when the first has arrived at ℘. For the explanation see p. 89.

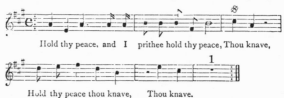

Hold thy peace, and I   prithee hold thy peace, Thou knave,

Hold thy peace thou knave,   Thou knave.

"Thou knave" will be heard *nine* times for every once the whole tune is sung by one of the voices.

I. "Jack boy, ho boy, news." See pp. 76, 91, *Taming of the Shrew*, IV, i, 42. This is very old, probably quite early sixteenth century (see Introductory).

For *four* voices. The second man comes in at ℘, as before.

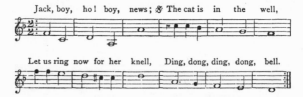

Jack, boy,   ho! boy,   news; ℘ The cat is   in   the   well,

Let us ring now for her   knell,   Ding, dong, ding, dong,   bell.

24. Three-man songs (corrupted into "Freeman," see p. 82). These were entirely different from catches. A three-man song is merely (as a rule) a song with *three parts*, e.g. two trebles and a tenor, etc. *Winter's Tale*, IV, ii, 41, and IV, iii, 285–327.

Here is a three-man song, published in 1609, but probably much older than that.

Transposed down a fourth.

There are two more verses of the same sort.

25. "Canst thou not hit it," *Love's Labour's Lost*, IV, i, 125. No more words known, except this one verse.

The tune is mentioned as a dance in an Elizabethan play, and is alluded to in an old ballad, "Arthur a Bradley."

26. Dances.   (Also see Note on Arbeau's *Orchésographie*.)
(*a*) Pavan and Galliard, "St. Thomas Wake," by Dr.
Bull (1563–1628), from *Parthenia*, printed 1611.   See p.
111.

Pavan (if played quick became Passamezzo).   *Twelfth Night*,
V, i, 200.

Galliard, "St. Thomas Wake," the *same music* but in triple time. *Twelfth Night*, I, iii, 127, *Henry V*, I, ii, 252.

Galliard, or Cinquepace.

(*b*) 1. Part of a Passamezzo, date 1581 (see Note on Arbeau's *Orchésographie*).   See p. 131, *Twelfth Night*, V, i, 197. Passamezzo, or Measure (*As You Like It*, V, iv, 178, etc.).

etc.

(*b*) 2. The first "strain" of a German Pavan for the lute, dating 1562.

etc.

(*c*) An English Haye, or Raye, or Round, date 1678. See p. 127, *Love's Labour 's Lost*, V, i, 148.

For a French Haye, see Note on Arbeau's *Orchésographie*. Tune only given (see Stainer and Barrett's *Dictionary of Musical Terms*).

It will be noticed that the steps of the Haye, as given in *Orchèsographie*, can be adapted to this tune. The dotted minim value of this corresponds with the semibreve value of the other.

(*d*) 1. "The King's Hunting Jig," by Dr. Bull (1563–1628). See p. 121, *Hamlet*, II, ii, 504, etc.

(*d*) 2. "The Cobbler's Jigg," 1622. See p. 121. This tune was known in Holland as "Engelslapperken" (English Cobbler). It appears in two Dutch books, *Bellerophon* (Amsterdam 1622), and *Nederlandtsche Gedenkclanck* (1626). It may be older, for Mr. Arthur de Greef, in his "Quatre vieilles chansons flamandes" for orchestra, uses an almost identical tune, which he connects with the Duke of Alva's Statue, date 1569.

(e) 1. An English Morris, 1650. See p. 129, *All 's Well that Ends Well*, II, ii, 20, etc.

(e) 2. Italian Moresca, by Claudio Monteverde, from his opera *Orfeo*, 1608. This at all events must have had a different step to the Morisque of Arbeau. (See Note on the *Orchésographie*.)

This dance is certainly in triple rhythm, but the common-time sign is used in a sense long obsolete. It is a semi-circle, implying imperfection, i.e. two minims to a semibreve, not three.

(f) Part of "My Ladye Carey's Dumpe," *c*. 1600. See p. 124, *Two Gentlemen of Verona*, III, ii, 83, etc.

Then return to *. This is about *one-third* of it. The last
strain of all is the first here printed, but in *four* parts. The
authenticity of this version of "My Ladye Carey's Dumpe"
is doubtful. But a careful copy of the original for virginals,
dated 1510, may be found in my *Shakespeare Music* (Curwen),
p. 7, together with an arrangement for strings on p. 5.

N.B.—For Cinquepace, Canaries, Brawl, Lavolta, Courante,
Haye, Morisque, see the Note on *Orchésographie*.

27. Musical Stage Directions. See p. 159.

(*a*) Flourish, believed to be of Charles II's time. See p. 161.

Eight Trumpets.

(*b*) The Ancient English Drum March, revived in 1610.
See p. 166, 1 *Henry VI*, III, iii, 30.

APPENDIX

THE VOLUNTARY.

THE MARCH.

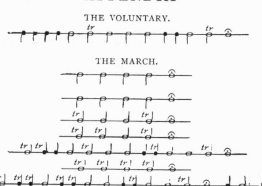

(*c*) Military March of the French "Gardes de la Marine,"
written by Lully, 1670. For hautboys in four parts. See
p. 169. Cf. 1 *Henry VI*, III, iii, 33.

Batterie de Tambour

Air des Hautbois

(*d*) A "sonnerie" of French cavalry, 1636 (Louis XIII).
See p. 172. I connect this with "sennet."

Boute-selle (i.e. "to horse").

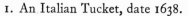

(*e*) Tucket. See p. 174, Cf. *Henry V*, IV, ii, 35.

1. An Italian Tucket, date 1638.

2. French Tucket, 1643.

(*f*) 1. Old French hunting fanfare. Perhaps may be connected with "Horns wind a peal" (*Titus Andronicus*, II, ii, 10). See p. 177.

(*f*) 2. The imitation (by violins) of a hunting call in Purcell's *Dido and Æneas*, 1689. See p. 177.

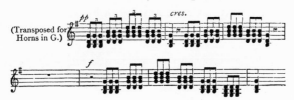

OTHER PUBLISHED WORKS
BY THE AUTHOR OF THIS BOOK

Music

Arthur the King (1902), cantata; words by Tennyson.

Requiem (Pax Dei) published 1912 (Novello & Co. Ltd.); performed Cambridge, Liverpool, and Harrogate.

The Angelus, opera, published 1908 by Ricordi; performed twice at Covent Garden, 1909, and in 1921 at Manchester, Leeds, Sheffield, Aberdeen, Hull, Nottingham, and Covent Garden.

The Merry Bells of Yule, for large choir (Novello & Co. Ltd.), 1898.

Vox Dicentis, for large choir, published 1919 (J. Curwen & Sons Ltd.).

Magnificat, etc., for double choir (J. Curwen & Sons Ltd.), 1918.

Anthems published by Novello & Co. Ltd.: *O Jerusalem, Look about Thee; Christ both Died and Rose; Behold, God is Great; And there shall be Signs; This is the Month* (Milton); *I will Cause the Shower; We have Heard with our Ears; The Merry Bells of Yule* (Tennyson).

Canticles published by Novello & Co. Ltd.: *Te Deum* in E flat (unison); *Te Deum* in A (full choir); *Jubilate* in A (full choir); *Te Deum* in A flat (for men); *Jubilate* in A flat (for men); *Magnificat* and *Nunc Dimittis* in G (for men).

Other pieces for men: *Charge of the Light Brigade* (Boosey); *Land of Little People* (Anonymous) (Novello & Co. Ltd.); *The Nights* (Barry Cornwall) (Stainer & Bell).

Published by the Faith Press: *Anthem for St. Andrew's Day* (full choir); Morning and Evening Canticles (for men) (not yet in the press).

Published by J. Curwen and Sons Ltd.: *Benedicite* in G (sixteenth thousand); *Magnificat*, etc., for double choir, in G; *Vox Dicentis* (for full chorus).

Also published by J. Curwen & Sons Ltd., settings of Shakespeare songs, published separately: *Jon, come Kisse me now*; *It was a Lover*; *Peg a Ramsey*; *Callino* (published by the *Daily Express* in their *Community Song Book*, 1927).

Besides over two hundred pages of octavo church-music mostly published by Novello & Co. Ltd.

Books

Elizabethan Virginal Book (1905) (J. M. Dent & Sons Ltd.).

Shakespeare Music (J. Curwen & Sons Ltd.). First edition, 1912; second edition, with an Appendix, February 1928.

INDEX

206